To Peter,

I hope you enjoy the book and we look forward to seeing you again in the near future.

All the best,

Wayne

Off Piste

with
Wayne
Watson

TTL

PO BOX 200
Harrogate
HG1 2YR
England

www.takethat.co.uk
Email: sales@takethat.co.uk
Fax: +44 (0) 1423 526035

ISBN: 1-903994-02-0

Alpine Experience may be contacted at Jean Sport, BP 307, 73154 Val d'Isère cedex, France. Tel: +33 (0)479 06 28 81 or email: info@alpineexperience.com

10 9 8 7 6 5 4 3 2

Disclaimer:
The information in this publication is distributed on an "as is" basis, without warranty. While very effort has been made to ensure that this book is free from errors or omissions, neither the author, the publisher, or their respective employees and agents, shall have any liability to any person or entity with respect to any liability, loss or damage caused or alleged to have been caused directly or indirectly by advice or instructions contained in this book or by the computer hardware or software products described herein. **Readers are urged to seek prior expert advice before making decisions, or refraining from making decisions, based on information or advice contained in this book.**

Skiing Off Piste is a potentially dangerous activity and you should only attempt it with a professionally qualified guide.

TTL books are available at special quantity discounts to use as premiums and sales promotions. For more information, please contact the Director of Special Sales at the above address or contact your local bookshop.

Contents

continued

Preface

TO ME the most important aspect of skiing is just being in the mountains. It is a way of travelling, of moving about in some of the most beautiful settings in the world. The mountains are a place of peace, beauty, and tranquillity. They are also a place of incredible power and unpredictability. Just being in the mountains is a privilege, and time shared in this environment with friends and family leaves you with memories that will last a lifetime.

Skiing is also a sport of grace, finesse, and power. It is an incredibly precise sport and to excel takes a concentrated effort, which makes progress very rewarding. Total beginners have their own 'thrill' level just as the extreme skiers have theirs. It is fun and a challenge from the very first day. And for me, even after 37 years of skiing, I still enjoy every snowflake that passes under my skis.

This book is about sharing with you a love for off-piste skiing and a quest for smooth, clean technique. I will also offer some of my experiences to you, both good and bad, in order to help you understand the beauty and the beast. My desire is to give you an idea of basic fundamentals in off-piste procedures and etiquette so that you can digest your own experiences and start to develop good off-piste habits. I will give you some constructive technical tips to help you deal with the many different types of snow found off-piste, so that you can fully benefit from the alpine environment. With adaptable technique, options in equipment, an understanding of safety procedure and etiquette, my aim is to maximise your potential and give you a basic knowledge so that your skiing is safe, and always a totally pleasurable and fulfilling experience.

Most of the stories used for teaching purposes in this book have taken place in Val d'Isère-Tignes and the surrounding areas. But, this book is about off-piste skiing in general. The attitude, approach and procedures that are needed are global and, as a skier, you will be able to visualise the events as if you were there.

Dedication

This book is dedicated to the memory of Giles Green.

Giles Edward Mortimer Green
February 9th 1961-May 28th 1995

Giles died on May 28th, 1995 after a two-year battle with cancer. Those of us who knew him will never forget him. He was larger than life, passionate about everything he enjoyed, and desperate to share it.

Giles started skiing with his family at the age of four. It was evident from his first days that he had an adventurous streak, preferring to leave the groomed trails to explore the unknown off-piste. He started off working in Val d'Isère guiding clients for Ski Val. Several years later he became one of the first British skiers to succeed in passing the full French qualification. With a growing reputation for his enthusiasm and expertise, Giles moved to Tignes to work with the E.S.F. Being in a 200-plus instructor ski school was not the ideal environment for a 'free spirit' like Giles, so he moved back to Val d'Isère and joined Top Ski. After one season he again moved on and became a founding member and partner in Alpine Experience, where he spent his last three seasons.

Giles was the inventor of the 'self-arrest', a method of stopping when sliding on steep slopes after a fall, and one of the most effective and useful safety techniques used in skiing today. It is now taught in many places around the world, passed on by Giles to those whom he met on his travels. Giles was known for his adventurous side, but at the same time for his dedication to safety.

Giles loved the outdoors. He was dedicated to cross-country running, cycling, hill walking, skiing, and mountaineering. But he was even more devoted to his family - an adoring husband to Bridget, loving father of Ghiselle, and at the time of his death, the unborn Isadora.

In his time of ill health Giles never complained, was never bitter, showed great courage, and always remained positive. For those of us who were lucky enough to have known him, he will always remain a great inspiration.

Chapter One

Off-Piste: A Re-birth to Skiing

I WAS very fortunate as a child to have grown up at the foot of the Canadian Rockies. I started skiing at the age of eight and my parents took me skiing each weekend and school holiday thereafter, and I could never get enough. Skiing had not yet become a major industry and still had a quiet, peaceful charm about it. The resorts did not have huge restaurants and bars but instead small shelters or lodges, where you could buy food and drink or sit quietly and enjoy your packed lunch that had been left in a corner while you skied. I used wooden skis and leather boots (the metal-Fibreglass-plastic equipment revolution was just around the corner) and feel privileged to have witnessed and participated in the tail end of that great wood and leather era. Needless to say that I was in heaven, aged eight in a winter wonderland, surrounded by snow-laden trees and the majestic peaks of Lake Louise.

At the age of eleven, Mike Weigle (now of Weigle Helicopter fame) asked my little brother and I to join the Lake Louise racing team, that at the time included an up and coming future downhill champion named Ken Read. My brother Dennis and I could not figure out why these young kids were climbing up and skiing down the same slope time and time again while we were free to go off and explore on our own. So, we graciously (if possible at that age) declined and continued to roam around in what, at the time, seemed a huge playground.

At eighteen I started teaching in the Lake Louise ski school for André Schwartz. André was a technical genius and he went on to redefine Canadian skiing at the time. What he taught me all those years ago is still the base from which I teach today. As time went on, we all became influenced by 'carving' and I turned my thoughts towards maximum edge and the perfect carved turn (yes, we could carve perfectly well without shaped skis). I moved on to teach for CMH and then coached a racing programme for the same Mike Weigle. But, by the time I was twenty-five, I was starting to lose enthusiasm for a sport that I had loved since childhood. The marked and groomed trails were all starting to look similar and, even worse, because of skiing in a controlled environment on perfectly groomed snow, each turn was starting to feel repetitious and an uncomfortable 'sameness' was creeping in. I decided to take a long awaited trip to Europe, desperately hoping that a change of scenery might rekindle my spirits.

As luck would have it, my good friend Lisa had spent a season in Val d'Isère, France, and told me it was *the* place to go. She organised my apartment in advance and in 1980, with my little brother in tow, away I went. I had no way of knowing what was in store for me and how this new environment would change my skiing life forever. Very soon after arriving I was introduced to off-piste skiing and discovered, for me, a totally new sport within a sport.

Dennis and I had never seen snow and a vastness of terrain like it before. The Val d'Isère-Tignes area is enormous. It stretches from the Vallon de La Sache and Les Brévières at the far end of Tignes, to the Col Pers and beyond at the Fornet end of Val d'Isère, with a huge expanse in between. With routes off the Col du Palet towards Champagny and Les Arcs, with Villaroger just down the road, La Rosière-La Thuile a bit further on, added to the then undeveloped area of Ste-Foy, the area becomes the best off-piste domain in the world. And we had just lucked into it.

We thought we'd skied everywhere, but we had really only scratched the surface of this wonderful expanse. And like most young skiers coming into this type of environment, we were probably lucky to have survived that first season. The town of Val d'Isère was a much smaller place in those days, and the 'Crazy Canucks' eventually met some people who had been around for a while. (We were far less famous than the same Ken Read led Crazy Canucks who took four of the first five places in the World Cup race in Val d'Isère.) We needed help and fortunately some experienced and very sensible off-piste skiers, T.J.Baird, who later became a colleague and my best friend among them, took us under their wing and started to show us a better way. And so the learning process began.

I quickly realised that conditions off-piste are ever changing and can change dramatically very suddenly. With 1,001 different textures of snow I was constantly experiencing a new 'feel' underfoot and felt continuously challenged. I soon discovered that to ski smoothly in these varied conditions it would be necessary to broaden my range of technical skills. This immediately gave my teaching and piste skiing much more purpose. Off-piste skiing had rejuvenated me. My skiing was challenging again and, as I had no real experience off the groomed trails, there was everything to learn. And it can be like that for you as well.

Through different eyes

My new friends helped me realise that to travel and ski safely in this environment was a necessary skill and an art in itself, and the sooner I started trying to figure it out the better. The mountains themselves can have an unpredictable nature, and for all their beauty can be cruel and unforgiving. They demand respect and a thoughtful approach, and you must be constantly in tune with all your senses. After hearing stories of what can happen, my friends and I equipped ourselves, and settled down to paying attention and trying to learn as much as possible, as quickly as possible. We had the evolution of the snowpack to study, which is critical for making sound judgements. It was necessary to learn about the local weather and the effects of the changing winds. Choosing the safest route and learning to spot, and then avoid, potential hazards and 'traps' is a must for staying alive. We had off-piste procedures to master, and my friends and I needed to learn to co-ordinate our movements and work as a team.

Photo 2, Plate section 1.

The learning of these skills in mountain craft is a slow and never ending process. Just being aware added a whole new dimension, turning a physical sport into one where your thought process and attitude are your biggest assets. With so much to absorb and digest, the repetition of the pistes suddenly seemed a million miles away.

Understanding that there are risks off-piste greatly added to the excitement and camaraderie I was experiencing. My actions not only affected my own safety but also the safety of others around me, and my friends felt the same. Those were great years and I made friends and shared experiences that will never be forgotten.

It also became apparent that out of this multitude of variations in snow, some conditions were much more pleasurable and safer to ski than others. Some conditions are what dreams are made of; 40 centimetres of light virgin powder without a track in sight or perfect spring snow without a mark left by another skier. Other conditions can be like a nightmare; a rain crust that pulls at your skis or icy spring snow that hasn't had a chance to soften. While some conditions are a wondrous delight, others are un-skiable and should be avoided at all costs. Snow can also vary drastically from one slope to the next and sometimes you may find several types of snow on the same pitch. But at this stage I was mostly skiing off-piste with friends. When we found difficult snow it didn't really matter. Everyone was strong and had the technique to muscle through it. If we arrived early or late on spring snow, no matter how unpleasant, we just dealt with it. If we took a wrong turn, we would turn around and walk back out.

But, in 1987, my off-piste took a serious turn when Pat Zimmer of Top Ski welcomed me to his team. We were six at the time, Pat and Jean Zimmer, TJ Baird, Erik Girault, Chris Souillac, and myself. Skiing with friends is one thing, but dealing with clients who need, expect, and deserve good snow was a whole new dimension. Being responsible for six other people off-piste added an intensity that wasn't there before. My awareness changed, and I started to see off-piste skiing through different eyes. Being surrounded by a team was an enormous comfort and made settling in much easier. What I had learned in the previous seven years was a good grounding, but was not enough compared to what was now needed. Under Pat and TJ, it was back to school again.

Now the necessity to eliminate mistakes was imperative. I was very lucky to be tutored by Pat and TJ. They introduced me to new routes. I listened and followed. I watched the way they opened slopes, and the way they taught teamwork within the group. And I watched their concentration as they observed every detail of their surroundings. They slowly taught me not only about where to go, but when. They helped me digest past experiences and analyse the effects of the wind and weather, which helped me develop a 'nose' for the snow. A 'nose' helps to eliminate certain areas and point yourself in the direction where you have the best chance of finding good snow. Once there, you can find visual clues on the snow's surface, which can lead you past the tricky skiing to the more enjoyable textures of snow. As the years have passed, my 'nose' has improved dramatically. I love to hunt for the snow and take great pleasure when I can lead people to the best snow available, especially when conditions are difficult and good snow is scarce. The challenge of finding the good snow while striving to be safe often upstages the skiing itself.

In 1992 my off-piste life took another turn. After five great seasons at Top Ski, I felt it was time to move on, and with T.J.Baird, Chris Souillac, and Giles Green, created Alpine Experience. We fortunately recruited Jean Marc Pic from the E.S.F., and the five of us started the 1992-93 season together.

It is now 20 years after first arriving in Val d'Isère and there is still so much to learn. I feel extremely privileged to be leading skiers off-piste for a living. Skiing with wonderful people in the world's most beautiful and spacious office, and going to bed each night and waking up every morning surrounded by mountains. And every day is different. The snow conditions change, the weather changes, and the light can change from one moment to the next. The season starts with keen anticipation and a wonderfully soft light with cold temperatures, and evolves towards the brilliant sunshine and festive atmosphere of spring. I am also very fortunate to work with a team of outstanding professionals. It really is a pleasure to come to work each morning.

Off-piste is real skiing. The conditions are ever changing and the skiing is always challenging. And with a little physical effort and by using knowledge and experience, you can get away from the crowds and the hustle and bustle of the resorts and lift systems. Out where it really *is* a different world. Off-piste skiing can take you to places of breathtaking beauty, tranquillity and solitude. It can take you away to places where the wildlife is still abundant. Off-piste can take you into the backcountry to untracked powder bowls or to slopes with perfect unmarked spring snow lying before you. Imagine standing in the quiet calm on top of a virgin powder slope, without a track or another group of skiers in sight. If you are already an off-piste skier you will fully appreciate this sensation. If you have never skied off-piste or feel that piste skiing is losing its appeal, think about it. Off-piste could be a re-birth to skiing for you as well.

Yes, you can do it

Off-piste skiing has a certain mystique about it. The views are breath-taking and being in the mountains, alone in a small group, with trackless sparkling snow lying before you is simply awe-inspiring. The quiet peacefulness has an electric charge to it. Your senses are acute as you try to stay in tune with this most powerful environment. You are in a totally different world and the only way to really experience it is to be there and to live it.

Unfortunately, many skiers think that off-piste skiing is beyond them, reserved only for the advanced and experienced. They have images of the steep and deep, of narrow rocky couloirs and other such terrifying places. These places do exist, but off-piste also has a gentle side, and the intermediate is perfectly capable of skiing off-piste. With a little help and the right conditions, the eight- to ten-week skier can enjoy the thrill and freedom - in flattering snow, on gentle slopes, and in stunning scenery.

Photo 3, Plate section 1

The first thing you need is the right equipment. Today skiers are greatly aided by technology and no one more so than the intermediate. There are a vast range of skis designed to make off-piste skiing much easier and these wider skis can help make powder skiing a reality for everyone. They give you a much bigger platform to stand on, immediately giving you a more stable, comfortable feel, which equates directly to increased confidence. The new skis allow you to stand up and relax, instead of feeling unsteady, rushed, and panicky. The extra stability allows you to absorb technical advice and gives you the time to concentrate on what you are trying to achieve. They are a great teaching aid and a must for anyone wanting to make the breakthrough to off-piste skiing.

Secondly, you need a guide. An essential part of guiding is not only to search out the best snow available, but to chose the terrain which best suits the ability of the group. In the case of skiers who are new to off-piste, especially the intermediate, forgiving snow and the right terrain are critical for a safe and confidence-boosting outing. Good snow and gentle terrain can help to eliminate the 'intimidation factor', putting you at ease and giving you a better chance to perform. If you are given the best snow and the right terrain, you are half-way home.

Now, all that is missing is the help of some basic but well-timed technical advice. You would be surprised at the effect that simple tips such as "keep your feet still in the snow" or "remember to breathe" or "do everything in slow motion" can have. Perhaps a slight adjustment on where you position your hands or how you plant your pole can help you break through and reach another level. Having an idea of 'how' makes life so much easier. Simple and to-the-point instructions can make an enormous difference.

Some of my most satisfying moments have come with skiers who are new to off-piste skiing. Watching someone who is apprehensive about a certain situation deal with it, and control, if not conquer, their fear, evokes a tremendous feeling of job satisfaction. You can visibly see a change as one lifts their head and puffs out their chest with newly won confidence. To watch someone ski a slope in snow that they thought was well beyond them, then look back triumphantly at their set of tracks, with the joy and sense of achievement on their face, is worth a thousand words. These are moments that people never forget, and it is a privilege to be there to share it with them.

A couple of seasons ago, I had a group of six friends aged between 40 and 50, who had never skied off-piste before. I met them the night before at the shop (Jean Sports) to discuss what type of previous skiing experience they had. It turned out that they were all in the same boat, about eight weeks skiing each under their belts. I thought to myself that these fellows would definitely benefit from some 'fat boys' so we decided that they should hire the widest of the off-piste skis for the occasion. I was really looking forward to guiding them as they were very keen and had no idea of what to expect. I told them to relax (it is amazing the state that people can worry themselves into) and get a good night's sleep (they looked like potential party-goers), and I'd see them in the morning.

When we met the next morning they were very excited, but also apprehensive about whether or not they were up to the job. I told them not to worry and to leave it to me. I really wanted them to savour their first taste of off-piste skiing, with a combination of good snow with easy terrain and astounding scenery. So, I decided on the spectacular Fornet sector. My plan was for a trip over the Col Pers and down the gentle northern slopes to the valley floor, and then out through the adventurous Gorge du Malpasset. The back bowl is vast, with extremely wide and gentle slopes - nothing at all intimidating. The most difficult parts would be the traverse to the Col and the exit through the gorge. Taken with care, both would greatly add to the adventure and should not cause any problems.

En route to the Fornet I would have a chance to warm them up on the piste and get an idea of how they really skied. With inexperienced skiers your margin for error is much smaller, and I needed to be sure that they were all capable of the outing I had planned before venturing off-piste.

Satisfied, we arrived at the starting point for the traverse, about 500 metres from the Col, and I explained the importance of spreading out and keeping a good distance between one another. It was necessary for them to go slowly, as the wider skis are more difficult to grip with than traditional skis, making the traverse a little trickier. One by one they arrived at the Col, and had their first view of the beautiful panorama beyond. We were early and rewarded by being the only people in sight, so we spent a few minutes on top to relish the moment.

We passed over the Col and side-slipped down the entrance. The snow was about 15cm deep, but not as easy as I had anticipated. There had been a little wind that had slightly compacted the surface of the snow. No problem for an experienced skier but possibly intimidating for a first-timer, and I was thankful for the wider skis as today they would definitely make a difference. We discussed the snow conditions and what to expect, and I gave them a few tips to help them on their way. I explained the position they needed to be in before initiating the turn, and to be patient and allow the turn to develop. I set off and skied about 20 metres, giving them an easy target and doing my best to demonstrate calm controlled skiing. Predictably, their first turns were a little ragged. A couple of them just couldn't get their skis pivoting and shot straight down leaving figure 11's. Time for some more coaching.

After a few more pitches they were gaining confidence as the lads were getting a feel for the snow conditions and an idea of how they should be applying themselves. I started to lengthen the pitches, giving them a chance to link more and more turns and develop some rhythm. By the time we arrived at the bottom and looked back up the tracks, each skier was grinning from ear to ear. The story of their progress was etched in the snow, starting with figure 11's, to progressively rounder and tighter tracks. These boys were seriously proud of themselves, and rightly so.

Next up was our trip through the impressive gorge. The gorge is where the Isère River flows from its source high above on the glacier. During the winter avalanches fill the gorge with snow, and some winters there is enough snow accumulating to build a natural snow bridge above the rushing water underneath. Usually there are a few gaps or holes where you can look down into beautifully still pools or the swift current. The snow bridges are quite safe at the right time of the season or the right time of day, but you must be careful when passing the holes. If you were to fall in a pool, at best you would get cold and wet and have a miserable 20 to 30 minute trip back to a warm shelter. At worst, you could be swept underneath the snow bridge and trapped by the current.

We made our way down through the gorge, taking in the scenery and searching for wildlife with the soothing sound of the rushing water in the background. Then towards the exit of the gorge we spotted a big herd of chamois above us. This sighting enhanced an already wonderful ambience and I couldn't have hoped for more.

At the bottom I had a group of newly confirmed off-piste skiers. They had dealt with their first traverse (experienced off-piste skiers will know that traversing can be the most difficult part of the day), and had experienced the stunning view in solitude from the top of the Col Pers. They had laid their first set of powder tracks, and conquered their initial fears. They gained confidence in their skiing and topped it all off with an adventurous exit through the beautiful Gorge du Malpasset under the watchful eyes of the chamois. And they had certainly dispelled the myth that you need to be an expert to ski off-piste.

If you are a skier, you too *can* do it. All you need is a little sense of adventure and some determination. With the help of a pair of off-piste skis, some technical advice and encouragement, and well-chosen snow and terrain, you will be the one enjoying the thrills of off-piste skiing.

A Touch of the Wildlife

One of the real delights of off-piste skiing is coming into contact with the area's wild animals. An off-piste morning where we do not have a sighting is an exception rather than a rule. Considering that Val d'Isère turns into a town of over twenty thousand at peak times, added to roughly the same number in Tignes, and we are fortunate that the animals stay around.

The most visible animals are the Bouquetin (elsewhere known as Ibex, and related to the antelope) with its tall curved horns and the Chamois (related to the goat) with its much shorter curving horns. In long settled periods in the winter, they may disappear high up the mountains, but come back down when storms close in or during periods of extremely low temperatures. At the other end of the size scale are the red squirrels that roam about in the larch forests.

There are also the tunnel-dwelling marmots, which hibernate during the long winter months. In spring they come out to sun themselves, and delight all onlookers with their playfulness. An adult stands guard and keeps an eye (they have 300 degrees of vision) on events both in the air and on the ground. They have a whistle to warn of attacks from the air, and another distinct whistle for danger coming at ground level. Those marmots that survive hibernation, and are fortunate or skilled enough to avoid the eagles and foxes, may live up to 20 years-of-age.

You will often see tracks in the snow that tell of the passing of a huge white hare. But, it is a real privilege to spot one of these rarely-seen hares that has camouflaged itself in a coat of beautiful white fur. Sightings of wolves are even rarer, but they are on the increase.

The Val d'Isère area is also a real treat for bird watchers and the golden eagle has long been the town emblem. But our range is one of the few areas in Europe where the wingspan of the beautiful eagle is overshadowed by that of the huge bearded vulture, known here as the Gypete. This bird was hunted to extinction in the western Alps but survived in Carinthia and in the Pyrénées. Adolescent chicks were reintroduced into the Vanoise National Park and they have since prospered. The huge bird has no fear of man and has become a reliable forecaster of bad weather. One pair comes down from its high domain to quarter the woods between La Daille and the Val d'Isère village when it starts to become stormbound. We also have the beautiful Perdrix Blanche - related to the Scottish ptarmigan - in its white winter plumage. You can hear the 'grouse' of these lovely birds as they call one another, or complain as skiers pass their habitat.

To come face to face with these beautiful creatures on an almost daily basis only enhances everyone's love of off-piste skiing. It really is wonderful to move around in a beautiful snowy wilderness that is still home to so much diverse wildlife. *Photos 4a-d, Plate section 1*

It's never too late

Once people have tasted off-piste skiing, very few settle again for the routine of the groomed slopes. Their outlook and goals change, and with it grows a new enthusiasm. Unfortunately many skiers think the years may have passed them by. I often hear people say, "I'd love to try skiing off-piste but I'm too old". As soon as someone comes up with that line I repeat the story of John and Margaret.

John and Margaret did not put on a pair of skis until they were 46 years old. John was having some medical problems and Margaret thought that skiing might be something they could try as a couple to get John the exercise he needed. John wasn't too sure at first, saying, "Don't you think we're a little old to start skiing". Margaret in her subtle but persuasive way talked John into a trip to Andorra and away they went. They struggled through that initial phase, where it is totally alien, and then continued to ski a couple of weeks a season for three or four years.

I first met them in Val d'Isère about ten years ago. They were very keen to work on their technique and the effort they have put in since has paid dividends. Now in their early sixties, they ski between 50 and 75 days a year and I can take them anywhere on the mountain in any type of snow. They love deep powder and are perfectly comfortable in steep couloirs. There is never a complaint if we need to carry our skis on our shoulders and walk up a ridge for 30 minutes. John often skis at the back making sure that everyone is managing and is ready to help anyone needing assistance. In fact, knowing John is bringing up the rear gives me confidence and makes my job a lot easier. If I pick up the pace and cruise the blues and reds at speed on the way down to lunch, Margaret is right behind me with a huge grin on her face. It gives me great pleasure to spend time with Grandparents who have the courage and the zest for life of teenagers. They are a constant inspiration to everyone they ski with, and give hope to anyone who thinks they are past it.

Another inspiring fellow I ski with is Doug Hooper. He passed his British Association of Ski Instructors Level 3 exams at the age of 62 and has gone on to spend five to six weeks each season teaching children in Italy and Austria. Now in his seventies, Doug still skis off-piste every morning of his two-week holiday, and spends the afternoons cruising the pistes and offering technical advice to his friends. He compares notes each day at lunch with Jacques Juranville, a retired French film producer who, at 73, skis off-piste six days a week for the entire season, from mid-November to early May. At such a venerable age, Jacques has decided that a day-off per week can't hurt. But he never misses a lunch at Les Tufs where he kisses the cheeks of every woman he sees, then theatrically sits down to the plat de jour and a carafe of red wine. To say he flirts with style is an understatement, and I sometimes think that Jacques missed his true calling and he should really have been an actor.

Photo 5,Plate section 1

It seems to me that over the years the complexion of ski resorts is slowly changing. There are now several different types of ski (or gliding) enthusiasts and a couple of contrasting ways to spend the winter skiing. You still have the younger crowd; doing their bar jobs at night and skiing during the day. There are many students who are taking a year out before going to university or doing a season after college before looking for a job. You still find the odd few who sleep in vans and shower when they can at the local swimming pool. And, of course, we now have the surf crowd as well, who for the most part have never skied before and are new to the mountains.

But, the big change is in the growing number of 55-and-overs, who are retired or semi-retired, who own apartments and spend their winters skiing off-piste. They have fallen in love with the mountains and skiing, and have been planning early retirement so that they can spend as much time pursuing their passion as possible. They have found a fulfilling interest that has made their retirement much more rewarding, and it is great to see.

If you would like to learn to ski, or would like to take the step from piste to off-piste but think you are too old, think again. These people are all living proof that if you have the desire (and the cash) - it's never too late.

Afraid of heights or steep slopes?

You would be surprised at how many skiers suffer from vertigo. And in no-way is it a problem for just the timid. It can affect anyone, and it is often the big, strong, rugby types who suffer worst. Some people suffer mildly and can cover it up so that you would never guess they had a problem, but others suffer to the point where they freeze with fear and simply cannot move. Each person has a different threshold before it sets in. Some may not show signs until it gets seriously steep (actually that sounds quite sensible) while others might tighten up on a red type run. But vertigo does not mean that you cannot ski and it certainly does not exclude you from skiing off-piste. It is difficult, but you can overcome it and control your fear so that you can perform. You may never be an extreme skier, but you will be able to ski slopes you never imagined possible.

I really admire the courage of people with vertigo. If you have ever experienced it or witnessed someone frozen with fear, unable to move, you will know how serious it can be.*

A lady called Lorraine emphasises this point. She was absolutely terrified, but she desperately wanted to get over her fear because she had a burning desire to ski off-piste. She was so serious about it she took five months off and came skiing for the entire season. She planned to ski off-piste most mornings and take afternoon technique lessons three or four times a week. (I told you she was serious).

Lorraine was actually quite a steady skier but we started her off in the 'initiation to off-piste' class. Here she quickly developed confidence in her skiing but was having problems on traverses, so I took her out a couple of afternoons and concentrated on some testing traversing. I would traverse below her and hold onto her pole for moral support and slowly she realised that she wasn't going to die. She stayed on in the initiation group even though she was technically much more advanced as a skier, and her confidence grew. Eventually, the time came when she was ready to move on to more testing skiing.

I was skiing with her fairly regularly now and was exposing her to steeper and steeper traverses, and taking her to more challenging slopes.

*I use the word 'vertigo' for convenience. I'm not sure exactly what causes the fear; sometimes, perhaps, it is an intelligent reaction to steep slopes when someone feels they are not technically strong enough to handle the situation. But in my experience, affected skiers often suffer on slopes that are well within their technical capabilities. More often than not you see weaker skiers who are fearless on slopes they should have much more respect for. Vertigo may not be the correct medical term, but whatever it is, with patience and caution the sufferer can make great strides in overcoming the problem.

She was handling the easier terrain on her own but still needed support in the more difficult situations. I was pleased and knew we were winning because her definition of 'difficult' was slowly changing. I continued to hold her pole on the tough traverses and on the steeper pitches, where together we would side-slip down. She continued to progress as the season wore on and by the middle of February she was staying right behind me on traverses but no longer needed me to hold her pole. She was also side-slipping steep slopes on her own until reaching a certain degree of slope where suddenly she would feel free and start turning.

By the end of the season she was traversing even the trickiest ones on her own, and skiing slopes that had brought her to tears and frozen panic earlier in the winter. She got to the point where she would give up her place behind me when she noticed someone else needing my help more than she did. I was incredibly proud of Lorraine and really quite surprised at her progress.

I think she had a love-hate relationship with the whole thing, as she was still frightened, but had the confidence and courage to swallow her fear and compose herself so that she could perform in what, to her, were extreme conditions.

Skiing with people you know is a luxury. You are aware of their strengths and limitations and not much amazes you. When you know that someone has a problem you can work around it, maybe by changing the itinerary or keeping the person close when they are in need. It is a totally different story when taking out new skiers. It takes time to evaluate people's capabilities. Technically you can have a good idea after seeing two or three turns but mentally it is another issue, and you can be surprised.

It was that type of situation when I learned the hard way about Peter's vertigo...

It was about 12 years ago and I had skied once or twice before with Peter, but always on gentle to moderate terrain. On this particular day, we had perfect (and I mean perfect) spring snow and beautiful blue skies. We had skied a couple of gentle runs to warm up and then I headed towards the stunning 'Tour du Charvet'. Great slopes, fantastic scenery, the possibility of spotting some wildlife, what could possibly go wrong?

The top two-thirds of the run are fairly easy and everyone was skiing well and thoroughly enjoying themselves. We skied across a meadow and I stopped just on top of the last slope that led down to the valley floor. A very impressive view and a very impressive slope. I had no worries as all the group members were strong skiers and I trusted their technical abilities.

I set off and skied down about 100 metres to the next roll. One by one the group arrived except for Peter who was standing at the top shaking his head.

Though I try my best not to make too much noise off-piste, something was troubling Peter, and after waiting a few moments I called back up the mountain, "Peter, come on down."
Peter hollered back, "I'm not coming down there."
I called a little louder, "Peter, come on down."
He replied, "I said I'm not coming down there."
My turn, "Peter, what do you mean you aren't coming down here?"
To which he finally screamed, "I mean I'm not f***ing coming down there."

Okay Peter, I get the message.

It was steep and warm, and I had to climb all the way back up to talk Peter into letting me take him by the hand, and side-slip him down to where the others were patiently waiting.

I had learnt the hard way about Peter's vertigo and have never again left him anywhere but right behind me whenever we approach a steep slope. After that day, as with Lorraine, I would take Peter's hand and side-slip with him until he yelled as if I were a nuisance "I'm okay now, let me go". I would then immediately release him and he would ski off as if he was never under a spell.

Different skiers have varying degrees of slope before their vertigo kicks in, and they also have varying degrees in steepness where they become free. It is like they are suddenly unchained; they can go from being petrified and unable to function one moment, to being loose, confident and fully functioning again the next.

Vertigo can be controlled and, in some cases, conquered. It should in no way be a reason to miss out on the wonders of off-piste skiing; you just need a sensible approach. If you do suffer from vertigo, make sure you tell whomever you are skiing with so that you can build your confidence and not be immediately thrown into a situation that you can't handle and will definitely regret.

Photo 6, Plate section 1

Off-piste - where does it begin?

Theoretically, you are off-piste the moment you leave the marked pistes or duck under the ropes. Ski resorts are only responsible for your safety on the marked runs and for the safety of the village or town. If you injure yourself on the piste the ski patrol will collect you and get you safely off the mountain. No questions asked and no complications. If you are off the piste, it is a totally different situation, and you may be charged a surplus that your insurance may not cover. The moment you leave the security of the marked pistes you are totally responsible for yourself.

Normally the snow on the edge of the piste is safe, but what most skiers do not realise is that you do not have to stray far from the pistes to get yourself into trouble. There can be terrain traps and hazards the moment you pass the markers and many avalanches and sliding accidents occur within 50 metres of the piste. I have witnessed many avalanches over the years that have occurred next to the piste, and three of these that I have watched from chairlifts, have been fatal.

Off-piste awareness should begin before you put on your skis, and off-piste procedure must start the instant you step foot outside the piste markers.

If potential trouble can be found immediately outside the piste markers, so can some wonderful snow. Some days the best and safest skiing you can find may be just to the side of the piste, or perhaps on the piste itself. There's a little slope in Val d'Isère, which is serviced by an old poma lift. It is a racing stade, which is not pisted after a heavy snowfall and, because it is protected from the North winds, usually has excellent snow. The Poma lift is short - maybe 300 metres - and you can do four or five runs in great powder with total security before anyone else shows up.

It is important to be prepared to enjoy the good snow that may be gifted to you on or near the piste. No matter how far you travel, the best of the day may be the snow that was closest to you. Often the goal with off-piste skiing is to escape the crowds and get as far away from the lift system as possible - but the further afield you travel the greater the potential risk. Apart from the stability of the slopes to be skied, you have the travelling to and from your destination to be safely negotiated. Sometimes cutting a track in to a slope in knee-deep powder or exiting a slope at the bottom can be riskier than the skiing itself. After a heavy snowfall you may need to be content with staying close to home, and not even dream of going too far afield. Four or five days later, after the snowpack has had a chance to stabilise, you may then feel comfortable enough to choose an itinerary that has some travelling involved. Patience is incredibly important as conditions change daily and the biggest question when guiding is not about where to go - but when?

A couple of seasons ago I experienced a wonderful Valentines Day morning that combined superb conditions on the piste, just off the piste, and as far away from the piste as I would dare go that particular morning.

It had been snowing and blowing most of the night, but dawn broke with blue skies and 50 centimetres of fresh powder. It was one of those dream-like days that promised great skiing, but because of wind and the accumulation of new snow, also demanded extreme caution and sound judgement.

I met my group at our meeting place and they were buzzing with excitement. I had a group of very experienced regular clients and my girlfriend, all of whom knew what type of morning awaited them. The saying "the early bird gets the worm" could have been coined with off-piste skiing in mind, and I wasn't at all surprised when they all turned up early. We made our way to the cable car, making sure we were on the first lift of the day. I love the anticipation in the air while riding the day's first cable car with 50 centimetres of powder snow waiting at the summit. Everyone was preparing themselves mentally knowing that today they wouldn't be warming up on groomed pistes. Immediately after exiting the cable car, I ducked under the piste ropes and signalled the others to follow. We were parallel to the piste that was about 30 metres away. Before us lay a pitch about 150 metres long and steep enough to produce face shots with each turn. The first turns of the day were extraordinary, and we looked back up at our tracks with huge smiles on our faces. What an incredible start to the day!

The previous night's wind was from the north, and I needed to choose a slope that had some protection from the wind, yet was safe from wind slab. No safer place than the piste itself and I chose the east facing Face de Bellevarde. Because it was protected from the wind, we had perfect knee-deep powder on the Olympic downhill course. Pitch after pitch we skied our way to the bottom, leaving beautiful sets of tracks as our personal signatures on the mountain.

Because we were on the morning's first cable car, first tracks on our initial run were easy. In the middle of the French holidays, 45 minutes later, the whole resort was awake and wanting to get in on the action. I knew that we would now need to work hard for our turns, especially if we wanted fresh snow and total solitude.

I thought of the Arselle sector and felt that it too would have been protected from the wind. Unfortunately, the lee slopes are also prone to *plaques* à *vent,* or wind slab (cohesive snow layer which binds well to itself but not to the layer underneath) and the slopes and line to be skied would need to be chosen very carefully. Usually after a big snowfall the lift at the bottom of the Arselle valley is very slow to open. If we walked five minutes at the top of the access lift and then 25 to 30 minutes at the bottom, we could separate ourselves from the crowds and be totally alone in a vast area. (For guiding purposes, solitude means you can concentrate on what lies before you, giving you a chance to choose the safest line to ski down the mountain. The last thing you need after a snowfall is an increase in risk because of people cutting back and forth above you. The decision was easy, this quality of snow was a treat and to ski it without anyone else in sight was a privilege worth working for).

We arrived on the summit and walked for five minutes, not only to distance ourselves from the masses but also to avoid a steep slope with an embankment at the bottom. A slide here with this much snow would be disastrous. We by-passed this potentially dangerous slope and arrived above a pitch with an even gradient and a much safer run-out.

The view was simply amazing. There was not a track in sight, from the summit all the way to the valley floor, nor from left to right across the entire mountain. The snow was sparkling in the morning sun and it was so quiet you could almost hear your heartbeat. To have first tracks and open a sector is always a special event, both for the guide and the clients. First, you need to have judged the slope safe to ski, but nothing is 100% guaranteed. Then it is up to you to choose the right line to ski and recognise, and properly deal with, any hazard that may wait. The clients want also to play their part successfully; they want to follow the various safety procedures, keep their tracks close, and most of all, they want to ski well. No one wants to feel that they have wasted great snow, or fall and drop a ski in the middle of the mountain. It puts pressure on everyone, but the excitement, sense of adventure, and common goal of a safe and well-executed descent makes for an amazing feeling of camaraderie. This shared vista and ambience is what off-piste skiing is really all about.

Because the wind can transport vast amounts of snow, adding to the accumulation of fallen snow, the entrance and first few turns would be critical. I tested the snow with my pole and 'cut' the mountain back and forth, and felt that it was safe to ski. Even so, with this amount of fresh snow my heart always pounds away in my chest with adrenaline. First tracks on a big slope in deep snow is always exciting, and to be honest, a little scary. No matter how safe I feel a slope is, I always think to myself, "I hope the mountain co-operates". I looked downhill and spotted a safe place to stop and regroup that was about 200 metres away. I pushed off and after a few turns felt the mountain was stable, but I still wasn't taking anything for granted. With sprays of snow hitting my face with each turn, I continued to ski my way down. One by one the clients skied down to join me, laying their tracks next to mine. There is something incredibly satisfying with laying a perfect set of artistic tracks, and we all looked back to admire our handiwork.

We took our time, and carefully studied the terrain before choosing our line. By avoiding dangerous 'domes' on the snow, and looking for good run-out zones, by staying on ridges and out of gullies, and by skiing and traversing one at a time, we did our best to ski as safely as possible down the mountain. *Photo 7, Plate section 1*

At the bottom we shared a thermos of tea and a bit of chocolate, soaking it all in before starting our walk out. My clients had played their part beautifully and the smiles told me everyone had enjoyed the experience as much as I had. The walk out was spent reliving the morning, and a half-hour later our excursion came to an end as we arrived back in the centre of the buzzing lift system. It would have been impossible to follow up such an experience; so I cut the morning a little short and we all said goodbye with that knowing look one has when part of a big secret. We parted hoping tomorrow would bring similar conditions but, we all knew that this would be a hard day to beat. I was also hoping that it would make up for the forgotten Valentines card.

This day was a good example of starting close to home and developing a 'feel' for the conditions. By skiing on and next to the piste, while observing the stability of neighbouring slopes, you can then make a more educated decision about whether or not you want to attack a big slope or travel off into the back-country.

Remember, off-piste awareness should begin before you put on your skis, and off-piste procedures must be followed the moment you pass the piste markers or duck under a rope. Sometimes the best snow is right in front of you and at other times you must walk for it. Enjoy it when it's easy; savour it when you need to work for it. Either way, powder snow is hard to beat.

A fear for the future

It always astonishes me how unaware and unprepared many skiers are when I come across them off-piste, or watch them from afar. It is often chaotic; people cutting back and forth, groups shouting and skiing big slopes all at the same time, skiers showing no awareness of what is above or below, far too many unequipped, and many with absolutely no manners. The places people chose to ski and the conditions they attempt them in are frightening. Most of this behaviour can be attributed to ignorance. People have just never been taught the do's and don'ts, and the how's and why's of off-piste skiing, and it is no wonder that there are far too many unnecessary accidents.

For me, the consequences of avalanches came to a head during the 1992-93 season, when a group of doctors and their guide were killed near Tignes, just over the Col du Palet on the route to Champagny. Besides being appalled by the deaths, I started to fear for the future of off-piste skiing. Each time there is a fatal accident there are whispers from the authorities as they wonder what should be done about reducing the death count each winter.

Since that fatal accident, I have been writing articles on off-piste safety, awareness, and etiquette, and Alpine Experience has been doing weekly slide shows and search and rescue exercises for resort staff and guests in Val d'Isère. This has been done with the hope of making a difference, in saving lives and in educating skiers (and boarders) so that the off-piste domain is a safer and more pleasant place to be. By promoting off-piste safety we are also hoping that we can help protect our privileged liberty to roam in the mountains, and not give governments reason to try to legislate our freedom away from us. It is, however, a long and slow road.

As a matter of course, my colleagues and I at Alpine Experience try to instil off-piste awareness in each of our clients. We ski and traverse slopes one at a time, explain why we are choosing a particular place to stop and regroup, explain the snow conditions and why this line may be better than the one further over. We train our skiers in the various safety procedures and etiquette, and give them a basic knowledge so they are aware, thinking for themselves, and participating. Active participation keeps them a step ahead and helps them digest their own experiences and thereby gain knowledge. We strive to develop good off-piste habits so that they become natural. And if the day ever arrives where there is an accident, hopefully their awareness and good, ingrained off-piste habits will help keep them, and the group, safe.

But years down the road, generally nothing has really changed. Skiers are still needlessly getting killed somewhere in the Alps after just about every snowfall. Perhaps it is even worse because the new skis make off-piste more accessible, and unless inexperienced skiers are being properly guided you can not expect them to know the in's and out's. The surfboard compounds the problem, as boarders can become technically good enough in three weeks to surf wherever they desire. It is impossible to have any appreciation for the unpredictability and power of the alpine environment in just a few weeks, and it is certainly not possible to develop mountain craft or etiquette in that short period. It takes years to develop good mountain sense and the learning process never stops.

My worries about the future were confirmed during the 1998-99 season when, for the first time ever, the off-piste skiing in the Haute Savoie was temporarily stopped for several days following a disastrous avalanche in Chamonix. There was an uproar of disapproval from the Mountain Guides who were not allowed to work. The decision was a drastic step that affected the livelihood of many people. Many, who were far away from the conditions that threatened the town of Chamonix, felt they could have carefully, and safely, worked if they so desired. During that same period, the préfecture in the Savoie gave thought to following the example set in the Haute Savoie. I am hoping that this precedent is not the tip of the iceberg.

Still, I shall persevere. I will continue to write articles and hopefully get my message across in this book. Alpine Experience will continue to give slide shows and run beep exercises, and most importantly, strive to teach good off-piste habits on the mountain.

Chapter Two

Avalanche!

OFF-PISTE SKIING is a potentially dangerous sport, and it is not for everyone. Once you accept and know what the possible dangers are, you can go about trying to minimise the risk to an acceptable level. If you then feel that the risk is still unacceptable, then perhaps you should not be skiing off-piste. But if you do decide to ski off-piste, it is then up to you to do everything in your power to be as safe and responsible as possible.

In the following chapters I will attempt to show you the good, the bad, and the ugly of off-piste skiing. I will do my best to emphasise the importance and effectiveness of the safety equipment, procedures, and attitude needed to make off-piste skiing as safe as possible. My aim is not to put you off the beauty off-piste skiing, but instead to give you a thirst for it along with a desire to do your best to be safe, responsible, and a pleasure to share the mountain with.

The two most common causes of off-piste tragedies are avalanches and sliding accidents. Even though both are major concerns to backcountry users, much can be done to minimise the risks.

There are three main contributing factors to an increase in avalanche risk:

- **An accumulation of fresh snow**
- **Wind**
- **A rise in temperature**

The deeper the fresh snow, the stronger the wind, and the more intense the rise in temperature, the more extreme the increase in risk will be.

La Grande Casse

La Grande Motte

Pointe de la Sana

Bellevarde

Rocher du Charvet

Val d'Isère

Crête des Lessières

Col Pers

Photo 1: An aerial view of Val d'Isère-Tignes from 35,000 feet.

Photo 2: *Delores, who introduced me to many of the classic routes, enjoying powder in the Mattis trees.*

Photo 3: *Denise being initiated to powder skiing in gentle terrain, wonderful snow, and stunning scenery.*

Photo 4a:
Hermine camouflaged in its white winter coat. Like the Perdrix and the Hare, they turn back to a protective brown colour for the summer months.
Photo:Jean Max Gunié

Photo 4b:
Young Marmots. Jean Max told me that the lighter colour of this one is extremely rare. His father who worked as a Park Warden for most of his life never saw one like this.
Photo:Jean Max Gunié

Photo 4c:
Male Chamois near Le Fornet.
Photo:Jean Max Gunié

Photo 4d:
Majestic Male Bouquetin surveying the valley below.
Photo:Jean Max Gunié

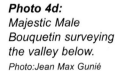

Photo 5: *A gentleman of 70 enjoying himself on some of the original shaped 'fat boys'. Notice the space between his tips. His technique would never have allowed him to ski in deep snow without the help of these skis.*

Photo 6: *Julian, Vertigo sufferer, age 65, enjoying deep snow in the Vallon de la Sache.*

Photo 7: *Gill having fun towards the bottom of the Arselle.*
Photo Wayne Watson

Photo 8: *Photo from near the top of the couloir shortly after the accident. The couloir had been full of snow and none of the rocks had been visible before the slide. They had been carried over and around the jagged, tooth-like rocks and exited through the narrow funnelling gorge at the bottom.* Photo Alex Pape.

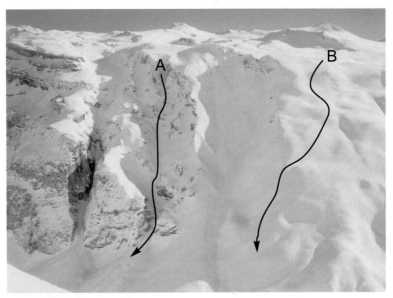

Photo 9 above:
The accident scene taken the next day from opposite side of the valley, which shows the flow of avalanche marked A. Note the route taken by the guide, who had lent them the skins and taken their photo, which uses ridges whenever possible, marked B.
Photo Alex Pape.

Photo 10 left:
Fred Foxon's face being uncovered as a client digs him out.
Photo Trevor Godfrey.

Photo 11: *Pete on perfect spring snow while on tour in Switzerland. Although the most forgiving of all off-piste conditions to actually ski on, it can be very dangerous to fall on.*

Photo 13: *Basic off-piste equipment.* Photo Wayne Watson.

The Self-Arrest Sequence

Photo 12a: Get your feet underneath you.

Photo 12b: Roll onto your stomach. If one or both skis are still on, the leg in the snow will become your uphill foot or ski and the leg in the air will become the downhill foot or ski. Make sure you are aware of where your feet are.

Photo 12c: Drag your arms down and under your chest, raising your body off the snow.

Photo 12d: Tips of boots are digging in and...

Photo 12e: You will come to a stop within metres.

Any one of these factors on their own can be enough to cause concern about the stability of the mountain. Fifty centimetres of fresh snow is cause for concern with or without wind, or a rise in temperature. Wind alone can transport enough snow on a sunny day, or during a clear night, to create isolated wind slabs (plaques). And a rise in temperature can be enough to overload the snowpack and trigger an avalanche. But, when all three of

The International Avalanche Risk Scale

1 Low

2 Moderate

3 Considerable

4 High

5 Very High

these factors are present at the same time, the risk is high. It is no surprise that most avalanches happen on beautiful sunny days, just after a snowfall that has been accompanied by wind.

Unfortunately, many avalanche victims are people who have spent enough time in the mountains to be aware of the basic signs. Understanding the implications of the various layers within the snowpack is one thing - it takes skill and only comes with experience gained over years of concentrated effort. But fresh snow, wind, and a predictable rise in temperature are obvious signs that any aware skier can keep track of.

Listening to, or looking at the avalanche forecast is the only way to start your day if you are planning on skiing off-piste. If the factor is 4/5, or 5/5, forget it. And if the factor is 3/5 caution must still be exercised. Don't forget, as well, that accidents can happen even when the risk is 1/5. The Risk Factor is always general, over a large area and there will always be isolated areas that may be cause for concern.

Most of the avalanche stories in this book took place on beautiful sunny days (guarantee of a rise in temperature), just after a snowfall that was accompanied by wind. The risk factor was usually 4/5, or bordering on it.

The question is not where to go... but when?

People who spend several weeks a year, or spend a season or two in a resort, are susceptible to developing a false sense of security. You see it time and again, and the price has often been way too high.

To me, there seem to be two distinct phases of vulnerability to the lure of powder snow and the sometimes moody nature and power of the mountains. **Phase One** is when young skiers or boarders (this really applies to enthusiasts of any age) who are capable but have no real off-piste experience first show up in a resort. They are fit and strong and generally looking for adventure. Powder snow is why they have come and many seem to have watched too many 'ski extreme' videos. They are prepared to go just about anywhere in search of fresh untracked snow, thinking very little about the dangers or the consequences. Youth often gives people a false sense of immortality, and the young sometimes think that avalanches only happen to other people. This is an extremely dangerous period and is often survived by luck alone.

The problem in this phase is ignorance. People just have no idea that there is potential risk and can unknowingly wander into serious trouble very easily. Some people get away with it, and some don't. But the trouble is that you only need to get it wrong once.

I went through this 20 years ago when first arriving in Val d'Isère, and looking back I know that we often skied in the wrong place at the wrong time. Fortunately, we were never made to pay for our mistakes. An American, who had arrived in town the same year as we did, was not so lucky. The poor guy was taken in an avalanche the very first day he ventured off-piste. He was skiing in the Les Tufs couloirs above Lac de Tignes when he set off an avalanche that carried him a couple of hundred metres to the bottom. He was buried up to his neck and spent several weeks in hospital with a punctured lung and various less-serious injuries. Everyone realised he was lucky to be alive and his accident served as a warning to the rest of us. Suddenly, someone we knew had become a victim, and this helped to open our eyes.

It usually takes an incident like this to startle the inexperienced into thinking about what they are involving themselves in. They are in a slide, or witness a slide from a distance, or someone takes them aside and explains the risks that they are taking, and they start to see the light. They equip themselves and start to make an effort to be careful and learn, and this is a giant step in the right direction. This new-found respect leads to a calming period where they try to do their best to learn about conditions and procedures. In the meantime they explore the area, learning the various itineraries.

Now they are heading towards **Phase Two**. After a period of two or three years in the case of resort staff or returning enthusiasts, a false sense of security starts to creep in (Yes, I've been through this phase as well). By now they have learnt various itineraries and are starting to feel they know their way around. And if, in their travels, they have been lucky enough to have no snow slide on them, they mistakenly think that this is a result of their newfound expertise.

This false sense of security that comes when you think you know more than you do, *is* Phase Two, and is a classic time of vulnerability. You must constantly guard against it, no matter how experienced you may be, or become. Professionals can be vulnerable, just as the inexperienced. Anyone given enough time can work out where the various runs are, but the biggest question when skiing or guiding off-piste is not where to go - but when?

Phase Two can often be seen in the behaviour of resort staff who have been in town for several years. Almost every season there is an avalanche that involves someone who is supposed to "know what he or she is doing", and too often these accidents turn out to be tragic. (I don't know why I say she because these accidents almost always involve males, and when a female is involved they have usually trusted a male partner).

Some bad decisions

Several years ago, we were having a predictably dangerous period in December and early January because of the cold temperatures that produce depth hoar crystals. These crystals have no cohesion and make for a very dangerous base for new snow to fall on. We then had a snowfall that was accompanied by wind, and the warning lights were flashing; rotten unstable base, 30 centimetres of fresh snow, and strong winds to load up the lee slopes and create wind slab. It was a time to be extra cautious and keep the travelling to a minimum.

During this period several of the boys around town had skied as a group for a few days, doing some of the classic off-piste routes in the area. The powder was wonderful and although the avalanche risk was high, they had no mishaps or signs giving cause for concern. Because everything had gone so smoothly they were led into a feeling of false security, and started to think of skiing further afield as the resort was being tracked out. On January 9th, 1998 they (Dave, Alan, Ken, Greg, Paulo and Rob) decided to tackle a day tour to the Pointe Nord des Lorès.

The day did not start so well. Dave's monthly workers pass had run out and he needed to dash about at the last minute and buy another one. With Dave sorted, they took the lift up then skied down the Cugnaï towards the Refuge du Fond des Fours where they would need to attach their skins and start their walk. Rob had trouble with his adapter binding not fitting properly and, fortunately, had to go home. Ken found that he only had one skin and for a moment it looked as if the entire group would turn around and abort the tour. But just as they were all about to go home, a guide, who was approaching them, asked what was wrong. He happened to have a spare pair of skins and generously offered them so that the lads could continue on their way.

As they worked their way towards the summit, Alan felt uneasy as the snow was continuously making 'whumping' noises. He told me later, "I was looking forward to getting off the slope we were climbing. I was a little nervous and just wanted to get to the other side, and start the ski down". After a two-and-a-half hour climb they made it to the summit, where they stopped for 30 minutes to rest, eat and drink. They telephoned Pete, who would have been with them except he had injured himself the day before, to tell him about the wonderful descent they were about to enjoy. The guide who had lent them the skins had caught up to them and they asked him to take a group photo. At about 12:30 they started their descent.

Alan says that he had only skied this run once before, in spring conditions, and wasn't really at all sure of the way. He assumed the others knew where they were going and when they arrived at a rarely skied couloir, Alan thought it was the main couloir, which was actually much further to their left.

It was an incredibly impressive sight. The couloir was steep and narrow with rock walls on either side, and it seemed to be never ending. And it was full of perfect knee-deep powder. They were all pumping with adrenalin and anticipating the ski of their lives. All the uncertain thoughts evaporated and the ominous signs were quickly forgotten. But what they did not know was that a south-west wind had been loading up the couloir and creating a wind-slab for the previous forty-eight hours.

They had a quick discussion at the top of the couloir:
- Is this the main couloir?
- Should we look for the big face?

Alan wasn't too sure.

However, they decided to stay in the couloir, feeling that it was safer because they had various rocks to hide behind.

Ken, the first to go, had just started to enter the couloir when Dave and Greg had second thoughts. They both felt that perhaps they should circle back towards the main slope to the left. Alan turned to them and said, "What are you going to do?" and after a moment's reflection they all decided they should stick together.

Ken had skied down fifteen metres and had tucked in behind a rock. Alan came down next and stopped behind the same rock. They were feeling a little more comfortable so Ken carried on and then Alan joined him. Ken continued on again for thirty metres or so and sought shelter behind yet another jutting rock. At this stage Alan stayed put. Paulo came down next and skied past Alan and joined the lead skier further down the couloir. They decided it would be better for Dave and Greg to carry on past Alan and join the other two further down.

Dave was next to ski down. He came past Alan and then skied out of sight. Greg started in and was above Alan's hiding place when the slope fractured five metres behind him. Alan was tucked in close to the rock when the slab broke away, but the snow underneath him started to move. Fortunately the slab was hard and it did not start to break up right away. It gave Alan a few life-saving seconds to react.

As the slab was starting to move down the mountain, with Alan riding on top, he braced himself and desperately jumped into the air, and off the sliding snow. That moment's action most probably saved his life.

When Alan landed the moving snow had passed him by. Within seconds the massive cloud of snow had disappeared down the couloir. Alan told me, "It was as if someone had pulled out a giant plug at the bottom of the mountain. Suddenly the couloir was completely empty of snow, and eerily quiet."

Alan shouted down, but got no response. He knew that Greg had been taken, and suddenly he felt totally alone. Disbelief came upon him as he thought that he was the only one spared by the boiling snow. Then another incredibly distressed voice broke the silence. Ken had been left clinging to the rock he had been sheltered behind. He shouted up, "Where is Greg? The others are gone". At this moment the dreadful reality dawned on them; the avalanche had taken three of their companions. Alan stared down the couloir. Ten seconds earlier it had been full of snow. It was now a minefield of sharp jagged tooth-like rocks. And his friends had just been carried through and over them at an incredible speed.

The guide (who had lent the skins and taken the photo) could be seen cutting over from the main slope towards the bottom of the avalanche. Other people were scurrying to help from the trail exiting the Tour du Charvet. Both of the survivors desperately wanted to help look for their friends, but neither could move - the couloir was void of snow and they were stranded on nothing but rock. Alan did not know what was happening below but he feared the worst, and the enormity of losing three good friends started to sink in. He and Ken stood 30 metres apart, each in his own nightmare, not saying a word. Alan managed to sit down, and to calm himself decided to take a few photos.

Photo 8, Plate section 1

Within what seemed four or five minutes Alan heard the rescue helicopter overhead. He felt relieved that people were already helping and that doctors were on the way. After ten minutes or so helping with the main effort, it flew up towards them and signalled for them to stay put and wait.

The next half-hour was spent in deep shock waiting to be rescued. Alan was trying to take in what had happened. Part of him felt excitement that being able to jump off the slab had saved his life. Another part of him was sick with fear about losing good friends. He thought back through the week they had just spent together. He thought of the picnic they had just shared. He thought of the group photo they had posed for with smiling faces only a short time ago. Then he remembered Dave and Greg's last words of doubt before skiing down the couloir.

Forty-five minutes after the avalanche the helicopter picked Ken up and lowered a Gendarme down to Alan. The Gendarme told him that, "Two are all right, and one not so good." Alan took this as positive news and was relieved to think that everyone may have survived. Five minutes later the helicopter returned, winched him up and flew back down to the Gendarmerie at La Daille.

As it turned out, Dave had died at the scene of injuries suffered from being carried through and over the jagged rocks. Greg came to rest ten metres above Dave, buried up to his neck. He had split his pelvis, broken a femur, broken one hip, dislocated the other, dislocated a shoulder, and had internal bleeding. Paulo was the last taken and did not travel the full distance, or at the same velocity. He came to a stop fifty metres or so above Greg, and was physically unharmed. He was in deep shock but had no recollection at all of being in an avalanche. Greg, on the other hand, remembers being carried over cliffs and rocks, by a huge volume of snow in a very short time. He could recall every cliff and rock of his horrific journey. He told me, "I kept being slammed into rocks with incredible force. I didn't want to be buried alive and suffocate. I just wanted something to happen quickly so that it would all be over ".

Photo 9, Plate section 1

Nobody at fault

This was a tragic accident and the names of those involved have been altered to avoid distress. But the truth remains that this group of skiers had all been in town for many years and had learned their way around. But, they should have known enough to be more cautious during such a dangerous period, and especially on such a dangerous day.

No one person was at fault. They were all very keen and as a group, agreed to go. There was a general lack of awareness to the possible risks created by a long cold spell, followed by snow and strong winds. And none of them were aware of the avalanche forecast. Alan said that the Gendarme asked him if he knew what the risk was that particular day. Alan replied, "No". The Gendarme then informed him that it was, "four on a scale of five."

Looking back, Alan felt that as a whole they were all too close together. To some extent, they had more than one person skiing at the same time. And no one in the group was aware of the 4/5-avalanche rating. He felt that as a group they'd had so many great days together over the years, without incident, that they all had a feeling of false security.

Hindsight is always 20/20 and everyone experiences situations where little things occur; signs that are perhaps trying to steer you away from disaster. These signs are easily missed, or ignored. The group's excitement totally outweighed the subtle warning signs at the start to the day. And their adrenalin and anticipation definitely blinded them to the obvious dangers that were present.

All of the survivors still ski. But none of them go off-piste regularly.

Same old story

Unfortunately, this Phase Two scenario is all too familiar. Many avalanche victims are young but have spent enough time in the mountains to understand the risks. During the winter of 1998-99, which will long be remembered for the tragic avalanches in Austria and France, Val d'Isère saw several accidents involving people who had spent several seasons in the resort.

One such accident took place not long after the big storms. Again, instability was not only predictable, but also quite extreme. A group of young surfers decided to head off-piste into an area known as the Super Spatule. This is a notoriously tricky area full of natural terrain hazards, and not the place you want to be when the avalanche risk is high. They triggered a slide, and although one very accomplished boarder managed to surf out of the slide, two were not so fortunate. They were taken and did not survive. This was another tragic example of being on the wrong slope at the wrong time.

The two who were killed were very popular in town and this avalanche shocked many of the young local ski and board enthusiasts. One long time off-piste skier decided 'enough was enough' and attempted to try to do something about it. He organised a video and slide presentation and had various professionals come and explain some of the basics of off-piste awareness and procedures. One of the pisteurs who was at the scene talked about the horrors of digging out the dead bodies. It was an excellent idea and had a strong impact on the young people who were new in town, and was a timely reminder for those who were becoming a little 'cocky'. Perhaps that evening helped some "phase one" candidates to avoid becoming victims themselves and helped remind the more experienced that accidents do happen.

These avalanches were tragic. People were killed and they will never be replaced. Those who witness this type of accident will never be the same again. But what would be even more tragic would be the rest of us not learning from these experiences.

Chased by the Dragon

Fred Foxon has been skiing in the Alps for years, and is the author of a book on technique entitled '*Skiing*', published by Crowood Sports Guides. Fred has been kind enough to let me use his avalanche story so that it may help others to realise the importance of safe skiing practice. Here, in Fred's own words, is his story of what it is like to be taken by an avalanche.

Wednesday 1st February 1995 was always going to be a memorable day. Blue skies, powder, and a group of keen off-piste skiers.

First descent's a steep, narrow gully opening onto an open face. Lots of snow in it, so I spend 10 minutes checking it out. Steep but stable, so I'll tail-end in case anyone loses a ski and ends up below it.

The group ski it one by one and park to one side beneath an outcrop. They're all down, standing in the crisp sunshine, reviewing their tracks. Time to leave my vantage point and join them.

First turn's a right-hander. Snow's heavy but consistent. A strong un-weighting, then the skis steer smoothly the rest of the way. Turn two rebounds easily from the first. I'm a little to the right of the gully's mid-line, just above some rocks. Traverse a little, then into turn three. Need to kick off harder this time, as there's no rebound. Pole-plant, up, and . .

No quick, shrieking terror, this; rather, a slow, gut-churning horror as

I realise what's happening. Looking up to my left as the turn begins, I see the slope start to bulge. Like the ocean heaving itself into a roller, a not-yet-cresting wave of 30 tonnes of snow is breaking loose above me.

That momentary glance conveys volumes. Both the fact of the avalanche and its scale. Alongside a sense of unreality is the realisation that this isn't just dangerous, it's deadly. But there's no time to contemplate mortality - not yet.

Two days later looking back down the gully I asked myself if I'd straight-line it. No way. But in that frozen moment, a single thought prevails - stall the turn in the fall-line, take it straight, the faster the better, get the hell away from this lethal juggernaut bearing down from above.

Next moment I'm blind, inside the snow cloud kicked up by the avalanche release. The same instant I realise I'm rooted to the spot, wedged by two huge slabs of snow. I'm standing on the downhill slab, but the uphill one has ridden over my ski tails. Although the whole ensemble is accelerating downhill, it's impossible to move or even fall over. The first of many chances that save my life. If I'd fallen then, I'd have been under all those tonnes of grinding, moving snow.

I'm aware of bumping and rumbling as the slab I'm standing on trundles downhill. No indication of speed, except the ride's getting rougher; nor of duration, as adrenalin-heightened impressions dilate in time. The whole roller-coaster ride probably lasts a few seconds; in the midst of the emerging maelstrom it feels like minutes.

Suddenly I'm hurled headlong forward, pitched over my ski tips as the slab disintegrates. After the shock, relief - I've ejected cleanly from both skis, reducing the danger of wrenched and broken limbs in the boiling mass of snow. Second dice-roll.

I'm tumbling head over heels as the avalanche accelerates downhill. But alongside the disorientation, a shred of reason tells me to tuck into a ball. Apart from reducing the leverage on outstretched limbs, there's the "muesli-jar" principle - shake the jar and the bigger bits come to the top. In a ball, with luck I'll be one of the bigger bits and stay nearer the surface.

It's hard to tuck in tight. The centrifugal force on my limbs, coupled with the viscosity of the aerated snow-mass inside the avalanche, demands a huge effort. And as I do, the spin speeds up yet more.

What, at the time, serves only to disorient, is also dice-roll number three. Lying prone within the snow-mass, the likelihood is to be pushed down and submerged beneath the debris. Spinning and tumbling keeps me in the turbulent upper layers.

As before, sense of duration is impressionistic rather than metric. The tumbling lasts long enough for me to recognise and attempt to respond to the dangers. It continues until my only thought is, "Please, I'd like this to stop now". In reality it's probably less than ten seconds.

Suddenly, I land heavily on my back, head downhill, arms and legs outstretched. A dull, amorphous whiteness means I'm not very deep. The snow is still avalanching over me, but its growling roar subsides; a silky hiss whispers into silence.

"OK - now!" Maximum effort, to break free or make an airspace before the debris hardens. Maximum nothing. I can't move a muscle. Like a fly in amber, I'm trapped in an enveloping, suffocating mass. The still-avalanching snow has packed into my nose and mouth, blocking my airways as far as the back of my throat.

And in that moment of stillness, realisation strikes. Having survived the avalanche uninjured, I'm trapped, suffocating, four minutes from brain damage and eventual death. No way anyone can find me, release me in that time. Recognition, resignation - the image of my children, whom I'll never see again.

That final impression marks the last moment when rational thought has any bearing on events. For with the realisation of dying comes a raging, overpowering panic. An adrenalin-driven urge to survive starts wrenching my head within the snow. With a power that rational-will could never master, the debris fractionally compacts. The blind craving of asphyxia drives my forehead against the snow, desperately struggling to make it yield.

At last, lungs bursting, there's space - maybe half an inch in front of my nose and mouth. Enough stale air in my chest to cough out the snow plug; gasp at the oxygen-rich air; choke as loose snow sucks back into my airways; head-butt the snow again to compact it further; gasp for life.

Still, mindless panic holds sway. Reason is reciting good advice. "OK - you're not dying, you've got air. Calm down, slow your breathing; minimise your oxygen demands and you'll survive longer". No way. In heaving terror, ribs straining against the pressure of unyielding snow, I continue desperately to gasp for breath.

Then at last - sound, movement, voices. So centred on my own survival, so engulfed in my own terror, I've barely considered the others. Thoughts of location and release have been submerged under snow and fear.

But now, the sound of digging; easing pressure; voices calling. But even rescue seems to last an age. Not caring if I'm hit with a shovel, the snow is carefully dug from my body; slowly and delicately cleared from my face. (Photo 10, Plate section 1)

Blinking against the sudden sunlight, my eyes adjust and focus. My first impression is of Graham, shovel in hand, looking anxiously down at me.

"Are you OK?"

"Yeah. I think so. Just get me out."

My left arm's free, while my right arm and both legs are still firmly embedded in the debris. He grabs my wrist and pulls. Slowly, reluctantly, as if being dragged from quicksand, I'm free. I climb from the hole and absorb my surroundings.

It takes a moment to recognise where I am. Knowing I've been carried some way downhill doesn't prevent the shock of discovering just how far. The spot where the group had parked is 200 metres above; the point where the avalanche caught me another 100 metres beyond that.

Afterwards, we try to establish how long it took from the moment of release to when it stopped. The consensus is between 10 and 15 seconds. So my average speed was 40 to 50 miles per hour.

That's why the snow was so densely packed. The distance

over which the avalanche slowed to a standstill was no more than around 10 metres. So the deceleration force was over twice that of gravity - about three times stronger than a car in an emergency stop.

At that rate, air is squeezed out of the snow like water from a sponge, packing the debris into a solid mass as it comes to a halt. No wonder I could barely breathe.

Two days later we return to the scene, to confront and learn from what happened. Looking down over the avalanche from the summit ridge, I see its true scale. Sweeping out in a shallow fan, its furthest edge is 400 metres below the fracture line; its width extends 75 metres across the slope.

Suddenly a tiny feature catches my eye. About 300 metres below, towards the right-hand edge of the avalanche track is a small hole. An eerie, dislocated sensation as I look down into the grave from which I was exhumed. Too many chances, too many rolls of loaded dice. Being well below the fracture line when it released, with many tonnes of snow above me; the rocks over which I'd somersaulted; the speed and power of the avalanche; my airways blocked with snow. I could so easily have died there.

Then something else catches my eye. The fracture line - a two-metre deep crown-wall, almost the full depth of the snow-pack. I need to find out why it released - what I'd missed two days before. It doesn't take long. On the open slope below the gully, the surface snow has been stripped off, but not to such a depth as higher up. Digging down, I find a loose, rotten layer close to ground level.

Dynamic changes within the snowpack have caused a wholesale migration of some of its substance, leaving an open, porous airspace surmounted by a coarse, granular layer. It doesn't even need a magnifying glass to identify these crystals. The biggest are about 4mm in diameter; their hexagonal, hollow shapes are unmistakable.

Depth hoar - an unseen, fragile hair-trigger deep within the snow. Caused by a period of intense cold, these crystals might have formed over a month ago. Since then, like a land mine they've lain in wait for an unsuspecting skier or snowboarder to release their tenuous hold.

None of the tests I'd done had identified its presence. Only a full-depth snow-pit would have sufficed. The alternative, relying on inference rather than observation, is to have a detailed knowledge of weather and snowfall throughout the season.

Certainly it isn't realistic to dig a full-depth snow-pit on each slope before it's skied. But I'd been in resort for only three weeks, and hadn't sought out enough detailed information on past weather.

In the final analysis, I'd screwed up - missed vital signs, or failed to check for them. As a result, I'd nearly got myself killed, and exposed my whole group to danger.

Afterwards, people asked if I had nightmares about it. Never once. But my real, waking nightmare is that it wasn't me in there - that it was one of my clients, maybe less experienced, maybe less lucky, maybe now dead.

It's an image that now haunts the mountains. A place of joy and beauty, twisted and transformed. For long I'd recognised its dangers; now I feel them in my gut.

No Rush

Everyone makes mistakes off-piste, even the most experienced experts. A lot of the time you may get away with it or even be unaware that you made a mistake. If you ski off-piste day-in and day-out, year-after-year, eventually something is going to go wrong. Maybe it will be because you made a mistake, or it could be that you were terribly unlucky. But one day, the mountain will not co-operate. The longer one spends in the backcountry, the greater the risk.

As off-piste guides get older, they become more cautious. Part of this is the natural mellowing effect of age, but I think most of it comes from experience. The more you see, the more you know that the learning process is never ending. There are too many circumstances - lots of which are out of your control - for you to be correct in all your decisions. And your respect for the environment and the possible consequences of your mistakes, continues to grow. You do your best not to take unnecessary risks and to be patient. You realise that the slope does not really need to be skied today. A friend once said, "Don't rush, the mountains will still be here tomorrow." And how true that is.

Do not be intoxicated by the lure of fresh powder snow and clear blue skies. Keep your wits about you. These are the days that are most prone to accidents.

What to do in an avalanche

Fortunately, I've never been taken in a slide and cannot give personal advice on what to do, or what not to do. I can only pass on what I've heard or read, what I can imagine, and what those who have had first-hand experience have told me.

If you are ever involved in an avalanche, hopefully you will have been travelling with the 'Golden Rule' in mind, and only one person will be taken. This would mean that the rest of the party will be safe and watching, ready to start an immediate 'search and rescue' with a good idea of where to begin.

But what do you do if that one person is you?

Before skiing a slope in avalanche terrain you should study it for a possible escape route, and ask yourself:
- Is there high ground to head towards?
- Is there a place of shelter to ski for?

My experience with slab avalanches is that when you hear the telltale 'whump', you have a precious second, perhaps two, before the mountain lets go. Do not waste that invaluable moment. Do not hesitate or stop, and look over your shoulder, wondering, what was that noise?

That noise is your warning signal to do something positive, immediately.

It gives you a split second to try to save yourself. If you are in the trees you may have time to wrap yourself around a tree (wishful thinking!). However, the chances are you will need to point your skis straight downhill, and ski for your life. First, shout out to alert the rest of the party that you are in trouble.

'The Golden Rule', when off-piste, is to never expose more than one person to risk at a time. See page 77.

Once you are heading downhill, depending on the shape of the slope, you may be able to head off to the edge towards high ground, or if the slide is not that wide, you may be able to ski out of it to the side. But first you must head down and distance yourself from the snow behind you before seeking safety off to the side. If you react immediately to the 'whump', and stay on your feet, you may be able to ski out of it.

If you cannot ski out and are trapped in the sliding snow, do your best to keep your wits about you. I often tell people that your natural survival instincts will take over, and you will fight for your life. Once you know your chances of skiing out are over, try to rid yourself of your skis. A sharp lateral twisting motion with the feet is the easiest way to release the bindings. Your skis will drag you under and increase the chance of being twisted like a pretzel by the power of the sliding snow.

Hopefully you will have removed your pole straps before skiing and you will be able to throw your poles away from you. This will also help prevent you from being dragged under or twisted, and will free your arms for the tasks at hand.

You often hear advice to "swim". Swimming motions with the arms and legs is your best bet to stay on or near the surface. In some cases this is possible. But sometimes because of the sheer volume and speed of the snow, there is nothing you can physically do, and you are along for the ride. If you happen to feel firm ground underneath you, push off for the surface.

During all this intimidating and life-threatening activity, try to keep your mouth closed and avoid sucking in snow. Snow will be everywhere and if your mouth is open, snow will find a way in. This will be difficult but keeping your airways clear is critical.

Once the avalanche starts to slow down you must be ready to take last-second actions to save yourself. Make a last effort to struggle towards the surface. Be prepared to get a hand in front of your face to create a breathing space, and try to shoot one hand towards the surface. And don't forget to move your head around to maximise your breathing space.

If you come to a complete stop and are still under the snow, after attempting to create an airspace there is nothing you can do but to try and stay calm; conserving your energy and your air. If you are equipped with a beep and you have companions above who are similarly equipped, and skilled in search and rescue procedures, you should have a much easier time staying calm. But being buried alive is no joke, and remaining composed is much easier said than done.

I remember speaking to Fred Foxon a few years ago just after his slide, when it was very fresh in his mind. He is a fellow professional and was equipped, as were the members of his party. I assumed that because he skis professionally and knows the importance of remaining calm that he would be able to relax when the snow came to a stop. When asking him if he remained composed to save his air, he replied, "Are you kidding, I f***ing panicked. I thrashed around like a stuck pig and bashed my head against the snow. And all I could think about was never seeing my children again. And you know what else? The closer I came to being rescued the worse it got. I could hear them above me, I could hear the shovels and I knew they had found me, but still I couldn't calm down. You have no idea how long ten minutes really is, when you are buried alive"

I have a horrible feeling that if ever put in the same situation, I might react exactly the same way. So much for staying calm.

What else could you do?

Often there is a firm surface underneath which the avalanching snow is sliding upon. And if the depth of moving snow is not too deep, Giles Green's 'self-arrest' technique (described in more detail in the next chapter on page 57) may just be a good option.

Giles' invention of the 'self-arrest' did not take place while sliding down the mountain after a fall. He was skiing the big face of Le Lavachet in Le Lac de Tignes, when the entire mountainside avalanched. Giles had lost his skis and discarded his poles, and was sliding along in the avalanche. He told me, "I lay on my stomach and pushed up with my arms. I could feel the toes of my boots starting to dig in and felt that I was slowing down. I could feel the snow passing me by and decided to be strong and hold my position, as it seemed to be working. The next thing I knew, the avalanche had passed me by, and I was stuck to the side of the mountain. Boy, how lucky was I?"

You also often hear people discussing various safety devices that are designed to increase your chances of survival if taken in a slide. There are avalanche **cords** that drag behind you and that will hopefully make their way to the surface, leaving a visual clue to your location. You can equip yourself with **inflatable balloons** to help keep you near the surface. They have a ripcord that must be pulled to release the air canister that inflates them. But these airbags can be a serious nuisance if accidentally deployed while entering a cable car. There are vests with a scuba-type **mouthpiece** that supposedly give you air for up to an hour. And of course, there is still the trusted **beep**.

But none of these techniques would be any good if you hit your head on a rock or tree. And even a small amount of sliding snow can be enough to carry you over a cliff. In big slides, especially powder avalanches where the speed of sliding snow can reach well over 100 M.P.H., you could be crushed to death or twisted into a grotesque shape. So, at the end of the day, the goal is to travel safely in the mountains. And your best line of defence will always be prevention.

Going for help

There could come a time when you may not be able to deal with the situation within the group and outside help will be required. When you are sure assistance is needed, make sure the person elected to go has a good understanding of what their mission entails.

- Arriving safely is a priority. The person will be in a hurry, but must remain focused and sensible.
- Know exactly where and when the accident took place. If known, name of area and altitude will help, and any other clues that may help pinpoint the location.
- Know exactly how many people are buried, and/or injured.
- Know the extent of the injuries.
- State of the rescue team. For example, how experienced are they and how are they equipped?

Chapter Three

Falling and Sliding

YEARS AGO I used to look forward to the arrival of spring because I felt it was the safer part of the winter. Even though you still have avalanches, the snow is generally more stable. I was developing a false sense of security that was shattered when I had my first 'slider'.

Trouble on the Bellecôte

I had a private group of men organized by 'Vertigo Peter' (see 'Are you afraid of steep slopes' in Chapter One), out on a boys' week. We all know that boys' weeks usually spell trouble, and I should have seen it coming. Peter had put together a group of six fun-loving guys who enjoyed their skiing *almost* as much as the nightlife.

The week started well and we skied off-piste in the mornings, followed by a long lunch, and then worked on a little technique (not enough as it turned out) and piste cruising in the afternoons. I was hoping to take them out of the resort for a day-trip toward the end of the week, so I slowly built toward it as the week progressed.

The planned trip is known as the Tour de Tarentaise. It starts by passing the Col du Palet in Tignes, then skiing under the magnificent North face of the Grande Motte and Grande Casse, down to Champagny. From there a 10 minute taxi ride would get us to a lift accessing the La Plagne area where we would make our way to the North Face of the Bellecôte. The Bellecôte is 1500+ vertical metres of impressive skiing down to Les Lanches. We would then take a bus to Peisey-Nancroix and ski through the resort into Les Arcs, across Les Arcs to the summit Aiguille Rouge and then down into Villaroger. In Villaroger we would stop for a feast of mountain ham, cheeses, bread, butter, pickles and, if I knew the boys, lots of beer and wine. It would then be a 30-minute sleep in the taxi back to Val d'Isère. All in all, the trip is a long and memorable day out with some stunning scenery, great skiing, and excellent local cuisine.

Because the Bellecôte is steep I had trained the boys in skiing steep slopes and taught them the self-arrest. I knew from experience that if I kept Peter close to me he would be fine on the Bellecôte, as he was the strongest skier in the group, and technically he would have no problems. But I wanted to be sure of the others. I worked on their side-slipping (if you can side-slip you can get down anything), stem-turns, and jump turns.

The big day arrived and we were ready to go. I asked the boys to go easy the night before and they had done their best, getting in around 1a.m. instead of the usual two or three o'clock. The weather was perfect, a clear blue sky and bright sunshine, and forecast to stay that way for several days. We passed the Col du Palet and skied great spring snow down to Champagny, surrounded by fantastic scenery and continued on into La Plagne. We arrived at the summit and made the traverse over to the entrances to the North Face of the Bellecôte. There are a few different routes to ski and I decided on what we call the 'Little Face Nord' because it is a little easier and safer than tackling the North Face from the summit. After entering the 'Little Face Nord', I cut immediately to the right and traversed so that I could check on conditions in the couloir. It hadn't been skied and the snow looked like it would support without being too hard. I thought the conditions seemed ideal and decided to give it a go.

Do not let the description of 'Little Face Nord' fool you. This was still a very impressive and intimidating place, and I had Peter stuck to me like glue. The couloir itself is probably seven or eight hundred metres long, with high rock walls on both sides and a relatively straight fall-line. We entered the couloir and I thought to myself that it was a little more impressive than I had remembered. I was relieved to have judged the snow correctly, as it wasn't too firm. There was a support layer with a few centimetres of fresh snow on top that would help slow someone down if they fell. Even still, I decided to take no chances and instructed the boys to side-slip the first hundred metres to take the bite out of the slope.

Further down it became a little gentler and much safer - and I wanted to get them down to that spot before allowing them to start turning. I looked up at the boys and said, " Under no circumstances are any of you to make a turn. We are all going to side-slip the first hundred metres. Remember, no turns".

Peter was behind me and seemed to be pretty relaxed; he had come a long way since that first time together on the Tour du Charvet. He could side-slip down anything and I wasn't worried about him. I allowed myself a little smile in respect for his accomplishments and was proud of the way he was handling himself. We had side-slipped about 20 metres when I noticed, much to my horror, Charles setting up to make a turn. I just managed to get "Charles, no t— " out of my mouth when he tried to initiate a turn. I could see by the way he was set up and his body language that he was not going to get his skis around. The worst turn in the world is a half turn, especially on steep slopes. And sure enough, Charles got his skis to the fall-line and no further. He fell back uphill and away he went...

I immediately yelled "push-up, push-up", and skied below him to try and stop him. If people even do half a push-up they will slow themselves down and make it much easier for me to stop them, but Charles didn't move. I was underneath him and side-slipping at the same speed that he was sliding. He wasn't yet going that quickly but being a big man he was going to be difficult to stop. I made my move and went for him, slowing him down and for a moment I thought I had him. But at the last second he slipped out of my grasp. By the time I got under him again he was really flying. I knew I had no real chance of stopping him, but with the rocks on either side I had to try.

He hit me like a train, and ploughed through me as if I wasn't even there. He knocked me out of my skis as I grabbed for him in vain. Suddenly, I realised that I was sliding as well, and in the same boat as Charles. Fortunately I was sliding feet first and I rolled onto my stomach and did my press-up. It was the first time I had ever needed the self-arrest in a crisis, and I was relieved to learn that it really did work. I came to a stop almost immediately and was praying that Charles had done the same. But I looked down only to see him sliding down the couloir at 50 miles an hour with rock walls on either side of him.

Eventually Charles came to a natural stop at the bottom of the couloir. His sunglasses had followed him down and, surreally stopped at his feet. He bent over and ever so coolly put them back on, and then waved uphill as if nothing had happened.

I bent over and threw up - sick from fear.

Peter was 150 metres above and totally freaked out. When I came back to reality I yelled up, "Peter don't move, I'll come and get you". One of my skis was at the bottom with Charles and the other was 35 metres above me. I climbed back up, collected my ski, and continued to climb towards Peter. It was a long way up and I arrived almost asthmatic with the adrenalin and effort. I calmed Peter, and then instructed the others to collect Charles' equipment that was spread out down the couloir, and to side-slip to the bottom. At this stage they hardly needed to be told a second time about not turning. I put on my ski and took Peter by the pole as we'd done many times before and, on one ski, side-slipped with him to the bottom.

The rest of the trip was a total blur. I was in a complete daze as I guided them on-piste the rest of the way. Usually the food at the end of the journey comes to mind, but this day I had lost my appetite, and developed an incredible thirst instead. We arrived at the Aiguille Rouge restaurant and sat down to sink more than the normal quota of beer.

I have mulled that day over in my mind many, many times since. Was it my fault or wasn't it? I had told them not to turn several times and if Charles had side-slipped like I had asked, we would not have had a problem. On the other hand, I decided to take them and one of them didn't handle the situation.

The problem is that it only takes once. And it only takes one in the group to make a mistake. At the end of the day, the guide is responsible for an off-piste group and no matter how you try to justify it, you always feel badly, and at fault, when something goes wrong. I still feel very lucky to this day that Charles arrived at the bottom in one piece.

What to do in a fall or slide

Sliding accidents are a very serious problem, both on, and off-piste. If you have ever watched someone fall and slide 300 or 400 hundred metres you will know how frightening and dangerous it can be. I do not have any official statistics, but would guess that just as many skiers are injured or killed in sliding accidents each year as there are in avalanches. Everyone will fall, the most experienced skiers included, and it is imperative to be able to stop yourself once you have fallen.

Photo 11, Plate section 1

Fortunately for us all, the late Giles Green came up with the 'Self-Arrest' as a method of stopping yourself sliding on spring, or firm snow, after a fall. And it is undoubtedly one of the most useful self-preservation techniques I have ever come across.

The self-arrest works whether you have lost both skis, one ski, or still have both skis on your feet, and it works on the hardest snow imaginable. Because the acceleration on a steep slope is phenomenal, you must react calmly, but immediately after a fall.

To execute the self-arrest after losing both skis: First, you must swing your feet below you so that you are sliding feet first. Next, roll onto your stomach so that you are face first in the snow. Once you are sliding feet first and on your stomach, you must then execute a press up. This raises your body (a slippery surface) off the snow (another slippery surface) and eliminates contact between the two. The elimination of contact between two sliding surfaces will slow you down but, more importantly, at the same time you will create a gripping effect with the toes of your boots and will come to a stop within a few metres. (Instead of trying a push-up with your hands directly under your chest, it is much easier, especially for the ladies, if your hands are above your head in the snow and you drag them down underneath your chest.)

The move is demonstrated in photos 13a-13d in Plate section 1

If you fall and still have one or both skis on, it is impossible to get totally onto your stomach. You will be partially on one side, with your chest and one leg in the snow. It is critical to be aware of this and what will happen to your legs during the press-up. The leg that is on the snow will become your uphill foot or ski, and the leg that is in the air will become the downhill foot or ski. Before doing the press-up take a millisecond to make sure your feet are not crossed over and that you have your legs under control. If they become tangled you risk spinning around, then needing to start the whole process again as you continue to accelerate and get closer to possible obstacles.

When doing the press-up make sure that you lift your whole body off the snow. This is easier if you make yourself rigid from head to toe. If you leave part of your body (normally the hip) in contact with the snow, you will slow down but continue to slide. Some ladies have trouble doing proper press-ups but I always tell them "you only need to do one". Remember that dragging the arms down underneath you from above your head is much easier than doing a press-up in the gym.

Practising the Self-Arrest

You must also be selective where you choose to practise. Find a short slope that is steep enough to pick up some speed but without obstacles for you to collide with. Also seek out a welcoming reception area where you would safely come to a stop naturally if you fail to execute the self-arrest. Look down and imagine where you will end up if you can't stop, and that should be a good indication of whether you want to try it or not.

Start off by sliding feet first with both skis off. This makes it easier to get on to your stomach. Then allow yourself to pick up a little speed (a little will do nicely on the first attempt) and then drag your arms down into the press-up. If you feel comfortable, try allowing more and more speed before executing the press-up. Repeat the exercise with one ski on and then both skis, remembering to be aware of what state your legs are in before pressing up. Once you can comfortably stop yourself, you will feel much more relaxed on steep slopes.

These next movements are optional but worth trying so you know how difficult it is if sliding on your back, or worse, headfirst. Try sliding down on your back and practise getting onto your stomach. Next, try sliding headfirst on your stomach and practise getting your feet below you. When you feel you have mastered these, try the acid test, head first on your back. You will need to swing your feet below you and control them, roll onto your stomach (still controlling your legs), and then drag the arms down underneath your chest.

As you will find, it is so much easier when sliding feet first. If you are skiing under control on a steep slope and fall, chances are you will have your feet below you. And if not, because you were skiing slower, you would have a much simpler time swinging your feet underneath you. If you are attacking in the steep, and skiing aggressively, chances are you will fall headfirst at speed. From this position it can be very difficult to stop quickly, if at all.

The self-arrest really does work and once you get a feel for technique it is actually fairly easy to execute. But it is definitely worth trying and practising in a controlled environment first. Once you feel you have mastered the movements you will rightly feel much more confident when skiing steep terrain.

Getting it wrong

A few years ago, I was training my group in the self-arrest on a short but steep pitch that had an excellent 'reception' zone in case someone failed to stop themselves. It was an ideal slope because it was steep enough to accelerate quickly and build some speed, so that my clients were in a realistic situation where they felt they really wanted to stop. The slope is accessed by a short Poma lift so that we could quickly do several rotations, and try to perfect the technique. I demonstrated sliding feet first a couple of times and felt confident that I could stop myself from any position.

My clients, however, made a couple of typical mistakes. A couple did not control their feet before pressing up, and end ended up spinning around. Someone forgot to stiffen their body from head to toe, and ended up leaving their hip in the snow after executing the press up and continued to slide. After a couple of tries, we were ironing out the kinks and they were making progress.

I then decided to demonstrate how to stop when sliding headfirst on my stomach. I skied towards the practice slope and without stopping, pitched myself headfirst over the edge. I already had momentum and when I hit the snow I was really travelling, and thought that this was going to be very impressive. But it took about one more second to realise it was going to be impossible to turn myself around, and to howls of laughter and applause (clients love it when you get it wrong), I rocketed face-first all the way to the bottom.

My mouth, nose, and ears were full of snow. Snow was jammed between my face and sunglasses, and stuffed down the back of my neck. Besides the exercise being highly entertaining for my clients, I realised that falling headfirst down a steep slope was not the preferred way to go, and have asked my clients for safe, controlled, non aggressive skiing, on steep slopes ever since.

Be aware of what lies below. If you have obstacles between yourself and the bottom, change fall-lines. If you still have obstacles below, ski cautiously, and give yourself the chance to easily get your feet below you and execute the self-arrest. Aggressive skiing often leads to headfirst falls with momentum, and believe me, it is not easy to control.

El Matador

Over the years I have had several people fall and slide in the wrong place. Some of them I have been able to stop, others have been able to execute the self-arrest, and a couple of times we have been lucky. Generally, however, if a sliding skier attempts the self-arrest and manages to get part of their body off the snow, they will slow down and make my job of stopping them much easier. When fallen skiers do nothing to stop themselves, it can be frightening, dangerous, and very difficult for anyone to stop them.

Ten years ago I was much better at stopping sliding skiers than I am now. As I get older I'm much more reluctant to throw myself in front of a moving freight train. Now, if someone falls and slides, I will look below and assess the situation. If there are no obstacles and a welcoming 'reception' zone, and I feel that they are not in danger, I'll stand back and let them slide. But if there is any chance of them injuring themselves, I have no choice and must try my best to stop them.

Speaking of increasing reluctance to stop sliding skiers reminds me of a story about an old colleague. He was skiing wonderful spring snow on moderate to steep terrain. His clients were all up to the task, but trouble arrived from an unanticipated source.

Ricky was standing on the slope with his group and choosing the line he wanted to ski next. Suddenly, from somewhere above came a hair-raising shriek. Ricky looked up to see this huge woman hurtling downhill on her back. His immediate reaction was to try to stop her, so he pushed off and skied towards the place where he would try to intercept her.

As he skied underneath her he realised that she was much bigger than he was, and she was sliding at a frightening speed. He knew that trying to stop her could cause himself serious bodily harm, and second thoughts about his bravery and wisdom were surfacing rapidly. Ricky quickly checked over his shoulder to survey the 'reception' zone, and felt she was not going to kill herself. Ricky's unfailing sense of humour then rose to the occasion. He held out his arms waving an imaginary matador's cape. At the last second, he slid back out of her way, and with gusto snapped his cape back over his shoulder and behind his head, and shouted, "Ole".

The woman grabbed at thin air desperately trying to wrap her arms around his legs that were so tantalising close only moments before, and continued to slide down the mountain. She eventually came to a safe stop naturally - shaken and stirred, but not broken.

Chapter Four

Travelling Safely in the Mountains

AT THE END of the day, the goal off-piste is to travel safely in the mountains. Off-piste skiing is a wonderful pastime and, for some, a way of life. But you do not want to get injured and you certainly do not want to be killed. Accidents do happen, and your approach to the mountains is all-important for your own safety, and the safety of others around you. The mountains demand your respect, and an effort to be as safe and responsible as possible. Here are a few ideas of what is required to protect yourself from taking unnecessary risks, and to avoid accidents.

Find the right person

To maximise your security and ensure that you find a good learning environment, I would recommend that you find a professional who specialises in off-piste skiing. He or she will have a never-to-be-underestimated local knowledge. They will intimately know the terrain and history of the surrounding mountains, and be aware of which slopes are prone to avalanche and under what conditions. They will also be continuously studying the ever changing snow and weather conditions, and their effect on the stability of the snowpack. In short, they will be tracking the variables that are critical in evaluating day-to-day conditions needed for making sound decisions.

A good professional will also be able to assess your skiing level: understanding both your strengths and limitations. Correctly evaluating your capabilities is essential for the guide to choose terrain and snow conditions in which you can progress safely. A well-chosen itinerary, skied at the proper pace, will give you a sense of accomplishment that will quickly build your self-confidence. A good professional will find the best snow conditions possible and put you on the right slope at the right time. He or she can take a dreary, flat light day and turn it into one of the best ski days of your life. The right person can make your holiday and ensure that you will come back time and time again to build on your experiences.

Finding the right person to guide you along the way can be easier said than done. The first thing you need to do when entering a resort is to find out who specialises in off-piste skiing. Once you have found a specialist, ask these questions:

Are they skiing off-piste daily?

It takes a daily presence in the mountains to assess the constantly changing snowpack and conditions, and to develop a 'gut' feel for what is going on. People who spend most of their time on the piste, and are then asked to take clients off-piste only after snowfalls, are being put in a very difficult situation. I would not want to be put in that predicament, and I would not really want to ski with someone who was being pressured into skiing off-piste on a once-every-time-it-snows basis. A daily presence should not be underestimated.

How many skiers per group?

Four to six skiers is ideal to maximise security, get the most out of the skiing and tuition, and to help create the best ambience within the group. A small group is manageable and you are capable of skiing places you wouldn't dare contemplate with a bigger group. Small numbers make it easier to keep the group's ability levels homogeneous, which helps keep the group flowing. This benefits everyone involved. The difference between six and eight skiers in a group is very noticeable, safety-wise, ambience-wise, and certainly enjoyment-wise. Four to six skiers also makes a good support team if anything were to go wrong. If the group you will be skiing in is too large - think again.

Are they fully equipped?

The guide should be carrying a backpack containing all necessary safety and first aid equipment. Many professionals are using radios with direct contact to colleagues, a base station, and the various rescue services (a mobile phone doesn't hurt either). In case of an emergency, contact with

Photo 14 Above:
Avalanche dogs in action. Pisteurs will first search the area with beeps. If no signal is picked up the next search is with avalanche dogs. When they are unavailable, or unsuccessful, the last resort is the probe search.

Photo 15 Left:
Keep your team on the move to avoid regrouping unnecessarily. Note one skiing the main slope, one on the second shorter slope, and one on the traverse.
Photo Wayne Watson.

Photo 16 Above:
Snow blowing off the summit of la Grande Motte indicating high winds at altitude.

Photo 17 Left:
Patterns on snow give and indication of wind direction. The wind has been blowing from right to left.
Photo Wayne Watson.

Photo 18: *The hole below is a frozen pond. This is a perfect example of a potentially disastrous 'run-out' zone. The snow will accumulate in the hole and surrounding embankment, known as the 'deposition' zone. Several years ago, a group of boarders overloaded the slope and one was taken through the ice by the force of the avalanching snow.* Photo Wayne Watson.

Photo 19: *Bystanders are kept back to allow the avalanche dogs to work. Too many people would disrupt the scent and confuse the dogs. If the dogs fail to find the victim, volunteers would be welcome to form a probe line.*

Plate Section 2

Photo 20 Above:
Moving from island to island. Two skiers waiting in safety on a rocky patch while one skier crosses the slope.

Photo 21 Left:
This couloir has several places to protect yourself: Behind the rock on the left, further down on the right, and behind the jutting rock on the main slope.
Photo Wayne Watson.

Photo22: *Probe line. By the time a probe search has been organised the victim will have been buried for quite some time. It is paramount to be able to mount your own search and rescue.*

Photo 23: *Debris showing the enormity of the avalanche.*

Photo 24: *Pietro leads the way as his group waits their turn. Skiing one at a time, a safer and stress-free approach.* Photo Mark Junak.

Photo 25: *Maintain your distance between skiers.*

Photo 26 Right:
A group well spread-
out and giving each
other space. A good
example of skiers
being aware of each
other's movements
and working as
a team.
Photo Wayne Watson.

Photo 27 Below:
Spring snow frenzy.
An undisciplined
group cutting each
other up and giving
each other no space
to breath. By the time
I could dig my camera
out of my pack, seven
or eight skiers had
already skied out of
the frame. Can you
believe this type of
behaviour in powder?
Photo Wayne Watson.

Photo 28: *Peace and quiet, and wonderful scenery.* Photo Jean Marc Pic.

Photos 29 & 30
Plants bloom in even the most barren of environments.

the outside world can be a life saving asset. Whoever you are skiing with should be asking you if you have a 'beep' (transceiver) and if you don't, they should be supplying you with one. Never ski off-piste without a beep and never ski off-piste with anyone who is not wearing one. If you are not satisfied that the person who will be guiding you is properly equipped - keep looking.

Most professionals who have been in the business for a few years will have a reputation. Some are known for their extreme skiing, others for their encouragement of the timid. Some are patient and some are more military. Some like to ski quickly and others prefer to savour the moment. Do not be afraid to ask hotel owners or locals what they know about various people (but be aware of chalet staff as their opinion is often coloured by who their present boy or girlfriend may be, or by who pays them or their company commission). Find someone whose personality fits your ability and desires. Discuss your goals with them. Let them know that you want to learn the do's and don'ts, and the how's and why's of off-piste skiing along the way. And you should feel comfortable with the goals of the group. If you are timid or suffer from vertigo, you certainly do not want to sign up with Mr. Extreme.

Once you have chosen someone, do not be afraid to ask questions in order to learn from your experiences and develop some mountain-craft. If you feel that the group is not being run safely – again, move on, and keep searching.

When you find the right person, you will know. You will feel safe, your skiing will improve, and you may become addicted. You will know that you are learning off-piste procedures and you will be gaining a healthy respect for the environment. And chances are that instead of changing resorts, you will want to return time and again to ski with that same person, and build on your past experiences together.

What makes a professional?

I have used the word 'professional' for a good reason. There are many qualifications that allow people to lead, or guide skiers off-piste. The word 'guide' in English means 'one who shows the way'. But because I live and work in France, I must be careful with the use of the word 'guide'. French Mountain Guides have a vested commercial interest in protecting the word 'guide' and consider the word to apply exclusively to them. But contrary to many people's beliefs, you do not need to be a Mountain Guide to be capable, or qualified, to lead skiers off-piste.

For example, I am not a *Union International Associations Guides des Montagne* (UIAGM) Mountain Guide. I am, however, a *Moniteur Diplomé*, which in France qualifies me to guide off-piste. The Val d´Isère-Tignes area has some Instructors who have devoted their professional lives to guiding skiers off-piste. They intimately know every square inch of their domain. They know which slopes are suspect and when. One of the most important factors in guiding off-piste is local knowledge, and these professionals have it in abundance. Pat Zimmer, the founder of Top Ski, and TJ Baird, my colleague and co-founder of Alpine Experience, both *Moniteurs Diplomés*, are two of the most knowledgeable and experienced professionals of any qualification in the area. Although neither is a Mountain Guide, when the snow falls and the wind blows, their advice would be valued second to none. For all these people who make guiding skiers off-piste their profession, I prefer to use the term 'Off-piste Guide', as a job description.

Not all of the 'guides' in the world's various heli-skiing businesses are UIAGM Mountain Guides either. Some have specific training for the needs of the heli-skiing industry and are known as 'Heli-skiing Guides'. The same can be said for the guides in the Snow-cat business. They have been trained for the demands of their industry.

When using the word 'professional', I'm taking into account all disciplines; Mountain Guides, Heli-ski Guides, and Off-piste Guides. The word 'guide' in this book refers to the person who is leading the group, or, 'the one who shows the way'. The word 'guide' does not necessarily imply that the group leader is a UIAGM Mountain Guide.

But at the end of the day, the qualification is a base from which the learning really starts and should continue. Safety is all about the following

Alpine Experience

L to R top row: Jean Marc Pic, Pietro Barigazzi, Olivier Carrère, and TJ Baird. Kneeling: Jean Christophe Souillac, and myself.
Photo Mark Junak.

I am very fortunate at Alpine Experience to be surrounded by an outstanding group of professionals. Our UIAGM Mountain Guides, Jean-Marc Pic, Olivier Carrère, and Pietro Barigazzi, are some of the most talented and modest people I have ever met.

TJ Baird and Jean-Christophe (Chris) Souillac have been skiing in Val d'Isère for well over 20 years and have a wealth of local knowledge and experience. Together we constantly discuss snow conditions and where to ski. Perhaps more importantly, we also talk about places to avoid. I never feel alone and know that I have a team of very experienced people to fall back on and help in my decisions.

Everybody participates and has valuable input that helps create a safe and professional working environment. We take seriously the faith that people place in us, and do everything in our collective power to respect that trust. Being supported by such individuals helps me deal with the stress and responsibility of guiding off-piste, and makes doing my job possible.

years spent experiencing everything that the mountain throws at you, and digesting the events and filing away the knowledge-gained for future use. How the guide uses this knowledge will determine how good they will become at their job.

Equip yourself

Being equipped is the easiest part of off-piste skiing. All you need to do is go into a good mountain/ski shop and buy what you need.

When skiing off-piste you must consider your group to be alone and responsible for its own safety. In case of an emergency you must be prepared to deal with the situation, as it could be hours before help may arrive. With this in mind each party member should be carrying as basic equipment, a backpack containing:

- a collapsible snow shovel
- a collapsible probe(s)
- a first aid kit
- a space blanket

As extras you could carry:

- extra clothing (gloves, hat, sunglasses etc)
- water (or hydrating fluid) and high-energy food
- pair of skins

Photo 12, Plate section 1

All party members **must** wear avalanche transceivers (beeps), and each skier should be trained in their use. Never ski off-piste without a beep or with anyone who is not wearing one.

By being equipped you are not only being responsible to yourself, but you are capable of helping others around you. It might be as simple as giving someone in need a drink of water or some sunscreen, or it might involve a life threatening situation such as locating and digging out an avalanche victim.

Learn to use your transceiver

Wearing a beep is easy; being skilled with one is an entirely different matter. A well-practiced expert is capable of locating several beeps within minutes, while a novice could easily stumble around for 20 minutes or longer before finding one. Fortunately, beeps are improving rapidly. They are much easier to use and are cutting search times down drastically. The new digital beeps have an arrow, which point you in the direction of the buried victim, and readouts that give you an approximate distance. This simplification gives the searcher something to follow and greatly helps combat the panic they may be feeling. Some of the new beeps have a multi-burial mode that homes in on the strongest signal. This will eliminate the confusion that comes from multiple signals when rescuers are searching for more than one victim. Hopefully within the next few years they will have perfected the digital beeps. The expert will be quicker, and an untrained person will have a better chance of locating a signal quickly enough to save a life.

Statistics show that the first 15 minutes after an avalanche are critical for the buried victim. A French study shows that there is around a 93% chance of survival if a victim is dug out in the first 15 minutes. From 15 to 45 minutes, the survival rate drops off drastically to 26%, and after 45 minutes the survival rate plummets towards zero. Some American statistics show a 50% survival rate at the half-hour mark. Other statistics show an 80% chance of survival if dug out within minutes. Whatever the source of the statistics, they all point to the same conclusion. Time is critical. And, you must be capable of mounting a search and rescue mission within your group, because outside help will not arrive in time. This means you do not have time to stumble around for 20 minutes trying to locate a signal. It means you must be skilled enough to quickly locate the victim, and then be equipped with a shovel(s) so that you can dig them out within the 15-minute time frame. Trying to shift snow with your hands or ski tips is futile.

Good habits and effective searching

Develop a habit of systematically turning on your beep before your skiing day begins. This may sound obvious but many avalanche victims have been recovered too late, usually after probe searches, only to be found wearing beeps that had not been switched on.

- Religiously check that each party member's beep is transmitting and receiving properly. Batteries may be running low; there may be a loose connection, or perhaps they have been dropped and broken. So always verify that each beep is working correctly **before** starting your days skiing! During the morning's beep check I *often* catch clients who have neglected to turn on their beeps, or find one that needs the batteries replaced.

- Practice safe skiing procedures. You should know exactly what the avalanche risk is, and plan your skiing accordingly. Use the "Golden Rule" so that if an avalanche occurs only one person is at risk. The others should be watching intently. Seeing where the person surfaced last can save valuable minutes, allowing the search party to eliminate the entire area above that point. Also, study the flow of the avalanche for valuable clues as to where the victim might end up. Wave motion over bumps and hollows, denotes areas where the victim can be deposited along the avalanche path.

- Someone must take charge and insure that all members of the search party have switched their beeps from transmit to receive, and that they are at full volume. Time is critical. If someone on the surface neglects to switch over to 'receive' mode, the other rescuers will be confused by the extra signal that is moving around on the surface. This would waste precious time and greatly complicate the goal of going directly to the buried victim.

The search procedure

> **Follow the three Steps :**
>
> 1) **Locate a signal**
>
> 2) **Initiate a wide search**
>
> 3) **Complete a fine search and locate**

Step One:

Locating a signal if you are alone

- Zigzag back and forth from the point where the victim(s) was last seen. If you are at the bottom of the slope, you must work from there.
- You should sweep from side to side for the first contact in case you are on the peripheral of the signal strength.
- Keep moving, slowly but steadily. Remain calm and focused.
- Mark the spot where you pick up the signal.
- Turn the beep until you pick up the strongest signal, and start your 'wide search' in this direction.

Locating a signal if you are in a group

- Spread out evenly across the avalanche path, but no more than 30 metres apart.
- Move downhill in a straight line until someone picks up a signal. Again, if you are starting from the bottom, work from the edge of the deposition zone back uphill.

Step Two:

The 'wide search' using an analogue receiver

- Your efficiency will depend upon how quickly you can detect a change in the strength of the signal you are hearing, so you must now continually adjust the volume control to the minimum audible value possible. This is where your ear is most sensitive.

- Hold your beep still and do not swing your arm from side to side. Always keep your beep in the same orientation to your body so that the motion over the ground is the only outside factor that changes the signal you hear.

- Until you start moving you can't be sure if you are facing the right way to start locating the victim. A few steps will tell you: either the signal will get louder (increase) and you can continue, or it will disappear (decrease) in which case you must turn around 180 degrees and start walking in the opposite direction. Again, by continually adjusting the volume to its minimum, you will arrive at a point (node) where the signal will start to decrease.

- Now turn 90 degrees in either direction and readjust the volume (changing the orientation of your receiver to the victim's beep will automatically vary the signal strength). Repeat the previous step to find out which direction along this axis you should be moving. Continue as before to the next node and turn 90 degrees.

- This process will continue until you reach a point where two steps in any of the four directions will give you a decreasing signal. You are now in the 'fine search' phase.

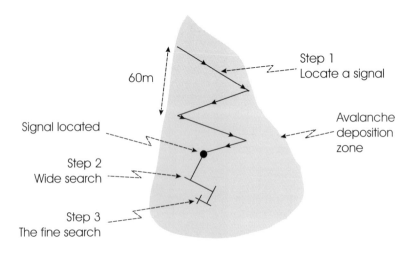

60m

Step 1
Locate a signal

Signal located

Avalanche
deposition
zone

Step 2
Wide search

Step 3
The fine search

The 'wide search' using a digital receiver

- Once you pick up a signal, depending on your beep model, it will indicate, using arrows, the direction in which to move and the approximate distance to travel.
- This method should bring you to the fine search fairly rapidly at which point you will either locate the victim immediately or will opt for the analogue method (if available on your model) to complete the final search.

Step Three:

The fine search

- With your receiver low to the ground, quarter the area, marking the extremities of the signal with a mark in the snow.
- The precise location should be obvious but a quick sounding with an avalanche probe will help locate the victim.

Whatever type of beep you have, practice. Have a friend bury one for you, and go look for it. Once you feel comfortable searching for one, try two. Remember, you do not need snow to practice your beep work. Summer is the ideal time for sharpening your skills.

If you have a chance to participate in an organised beep session, do not pass up the opportunity. Learning the proper search patterns and practising with your transceiver could be the best investment of time you will ever make. In an avalanche situation there will inevitably be some panic, and because good friends or family are often involved, this panic and sense of urgency can be greatly compounded. You must be consistently quick in training to have a realistic chance of performing well in the highly stressed, life-depending atmosphere of the real thing.

Buried Alive

A colleague at Alpine Experience, Olivier Carrère, runs weekly beep search exercises. He takes people out for a couple of hours in the afternoon and has an in-depth session. He starts off hiding one beep several feet under the snow and then progresses to multi-beep searches by burying two or more beeps. Because he demonstrates how to use the beeps he has had constant training and become very skilled at quickly locating a buried transmitter. All that practice paid off in the spring of 1998 when he came to the rescue of a buried avalanche victim.

Like many avalanches, it occurred on a beautiful sunny day. Olivier was out for a day touring and had chosen to take his group up the Barmes de l'Ours. Soon after starting the two-and-a-half hour walk to the summit, Olivier noticed another guided group behind them who had chosen the same itinerary. He steadily led his clients towards the summit where he planned to spend a half-hour or so, taking in the scenery, resting, and enjoying a well-deserved picnic.

The sun was particularly hot and was warming up the snow, even on the protected northern exposures that Olivier was planning to ski. He was worried about the warming effect and the decreasing stability of the snowpack, so he decided to cut the break short and move on. He carefully chose the safest route possible and skied his clients one by one to the bottom of the first pitch. He relaxed a little as they had safely negotiated the danger area. Olivier then noticed the group behind, who were now above them, preparing to tackle one of the steeper couloirs, so he quickly moved his clients across a meadow towards the next slope, a safe distance away.

As they skied the next pitch Olivier noticed a billowing cloud of snow in the air behind and above him. Instantly he knew there had been an avalanche on the summit and chances were that the group behind was involved. He immediately took off his skis and reattached his touring skins so that he could climb back uphill as quickly as possible. As he came over the brow of the slope he could see that there had been an avalanche and someone appeared to be buried. He climbed as fast as he could and was becoming increasingly worried as the searchers appeared panicky and unorganised. They were equipped with beeps but were obviously untrained in their use as they were moving back and forth across the surface without homing in on a signal. Olivier also noticed that they did not have backpacks, which meant they didn't have shovels, and therefore would be of little or no help in digging out the victim(s). By the behaviour of the searchers Olivier realised that it must be the guide who was buried. As he pressed on he studied the flow of the avalanche for clues as to where to start his search, and had a good idea of the most likely place to begin.

By the time he arrived about fifteen minutes had already elapsed, and time was now critical. He asked how many were buried and was extremely relieved to learn it was just one. Going directly to the place he had chosen, Olivier immediately picked up a signal and within a minute or two had located the victim. He assembled his collapsible snow shovel and started to frantically dig. The tension mounted as he dug and the bystanders were holding their breath, desperately hoping that he would find their guide alive. By now twenty minutes had passed and no one spoke as everyone realised what the outcome could be. When the victim's face finally appeared there was a collective sigh of relief and shouts of joy. Not only was he alive but he managed a thankful smile back up at the man who had saved his life.

Had the guide needed to rely on his clients he would most likely have died. In fifteen minutes they had made no progress in homing in on his beeping signal, and if they had eventually located him, they did not have the shovels to dig him out quickly. Being equipped is the easy bit - being skilled takes practice. Because Olivier is very good with his search technique he was able to find the victim as quickly as humanly possible, and assured that the memories of that glorious day were not tragic ones.

If I am ever unfortunate enough to be caught and buried in an avalanche, I believe I would have a better chance of staying calm, and a much better chance of surviving, knowing I had someone as skilled as Olivier searching for me.

On another note, Olivier had been out touring but this accident shows one of the reasons for carrying a pair of skins in your pack. Without them he would never have been able to climb quickly enough to have been any help. You never know in the mountains when you may need to climb back uphill. It could be to help search for a lost ski, help someone who is injured, get high enough to obtain a radio signal, or it could be a similar situation to the one Olivier found himself in.

A good mental attitude

If you have the right mental approach to off-piste skiing, your thought process can be your biggest asset. Accidents do happen off-piste, and if things do go wrong, you can find yourself in serious trouble. Respect for the power and the sometimes-unpredictable nature of the mountains, and the consequences of mistakes or bad luck, will help steer you away from taking unnecessary risks.

Staying in tune with all your senses, being aware of your surroundings, the snow and weather conditions, off-piste procedures, and the strengths and limitations of yourself and others around you, will help keep you focused on the task at hand. Be patient, and never rush. Give yourself and others around you time to think clearly and stay relaxed. Be willing to learn. Read, watch and pay attention to others who are more experienced.

Also, listen to your 'gut' instincts. The more you learn and experience the sharper those instincts will become. Digest your experiences and learn from what you do right, and more importantly, from what you do wrong. Everyone makes mistakes off-piste, the most experienced expert included. But as long as no one gets hurt, you can say that mistakes are a beneficial learning experience.

Stay aware and continue to learn from your experiences, as learning is a never-ending process. The knowledge you gain is there to be used to help you travel safely in the mountains and ski in wonderful places. Your attitude will go a long way in enhancing your appreciation for the environment, your companions, and your enjoyment of the skiing.

The Golden Rule

'The Golden Rule' off-piste is to:

Never expose more than one person to risk at a time

Every decision you make while off-piste should be governed by it and it is at the core of off-piste procedure. It governs how you enter, ski, and leave a slope, how you traverse, where you choose to start, and where you choose to stop. It should rule over all of your decisions in how you travel in the mountains.

If you are a group of seven and are unfortunate enough to be caught in an avalanche situation, the best scenario you could hope for would be that of one person taken and the other party members safe and ready to help. With quick beep work, and shovels to efficiently move snow, you would have the best chance possible of a successful search and rescue.

If, on the other hand, you had been bunched together and six skiers had been buried, with only one left on the surface, you are looking at a catastrophe.

To reinforce the point I often remind my clients before traversing or skiing a big slope, "Remember, we would rather be six searching for one than one searching for six". Keep this rule in mind at all times while skiing off-piste. It only takes once, and if your group is ever unfortunate enough to be caught in an avalanche, you do not want to pay the ultimate price. If you have conducted yourselves according to the 'Golden Rule', you will be left in the best possible position to save the day, or at worst, keep the losses to a minimum. *Photo 15, Plate section 2*

Be observant

Observation can be one of your biggest strengths. Stay in tune with your environment. Look around. There will always be clues to help inform you of conditions and warn you of possible dangers. *Photo 16, Plate section 2*

You can start when you look out of the window first thing in the morning.
- What can you see?
- Are there signs of wind?
- Is snow being blown from the ridges at altitude?
- How thick is the cloud cover?
- Is there a chance for blue skies further up the mountain?
- Have you listened to the local weather and avalanche report on the radio?

Once on the mountain your powers of observation should be used to the fullest. Look around for clues of avalanching.
- Are the slides recent?
- What exposure are they on?
- Are there signs of avalanching on all exposures?
- How much snow is involved?
- Are they natural slides, or are there black powder marks indicating that they have been set off by the pisteurs?
- Are 'stretch marks' appearing?
- Are they getting noticeably wider since you last past this way?

Also try to determine the direction of the wind. The patterns on the snow can give you a clue. When approaching snow that gives obvious signs, I often ask my clients which direction they think the wind has been blowing. Almost everyone first thinks of the overhang of a cornice and then applies the same theory to the snow on the surface. They are usually quite surprised to hear that they are wrong. In fact, the visual effect is the opposite. The raised side of the snow has actually been facing the wind. The more pronounced the shearing and overhangs the stronger the wind has been blowing. *Photo 17, Plate section 2*

Other wind indicators are more obvious such as snow blowing off the top of ridges, or out of trees. Knowledge of wind direction tells you where the lee side is, and where the potential wind-slab has been building. Knowledge of wind strength tells you more about how much snow may have been transported to the lee slopes. The stronger the wind, the greater the potential increase in risk.

Dan skiing beside 'stretch' marks in February. As the season progresses the snowpack will creep further and further downhill until it finally releases. These 'stretch' marks are often seen on grassy slopes that face the sun. ie. Eastern, Southern, and Western slopes.

Photo Wayne Watson.

More clues to stability can be gained by studying your skis as they pass through the snow while walking. While cutting a traverse I always watch what is going on around my skis. Are any cracks appearing or shooting-off in front of my tips? Is the snow around me collapsing? Are there any 'whumping' sounds coming from the snowpack? When these signs are present you need to reassess your situation.

Terrain Traps

Besides reading the signs to determine snow conditions, there are other indicators to watch out for, such as terrain traps.

Controlling the slope

One of the main responsibilities when guiding is in ensuring that the slope to be skied is safe. During periods where the snowpack is relatively stable this isn't such a worry. But there are days when dealing with fresh snow can be very tricky, and potentially dangerous. The guide must read the terrain and control the slope in front of them, from top to bottom.

The most dangerous areas are generally around a change of slope. An experienced eye can read the slope and have a very good idea where the slope's trigger point will be. When dealing with new snow near a danger zone you have three choices.

1. Avoid the area altogether, i.e. turn back.
2. Skirt around the most fragile area to avoid provoking the collapse of the snowpack.
3. Try to trigger the snow to avalanche by cutting the slope, or jumping on the right spot. But, if you choose this option, you must be sure the slope is controllable to the bottom of the mountain.

The last option takes an expert knowledge and experience in snowpack stability because the terrain must be read perfectly in order to cut the slope in exactly the right place. The goal is to create the fracture on the traverse line, or below it. The danger is getting it wrong and the slope breaking away from above, and being taken with it. If the slope doesn't go, you must then decide whether it is now stable and safe to continue, or, revert back to options 1 and 2.

Wind-transported snow binds well to itself, but not with the surface underneath, and so forms a plate, or slab, of varying depth. Plaques vary in size from small to enormous (entire face or bowl). The weight of a skier is transmitted throughout the plaque and can trigger the weak spot, which may be some distance from where he or she may be skiing or standing.

There are times when the plaques are isolated. They are in a certain area and will not affect an entire face. Cutting a slope should never be done when the plaque may be contiguous. Meaning, triggering a small slide in front of you may set plaques off for a distance on either side of you. A slope should never be provoked if there is any risk to anyone else on the mountain, whether they are below or to the side. The intrinsic fragility of certain snowpacks can cause a chain reaction that produces much more snow avalanching than anticipated, and this should be taken into account. Cutting a slope should never be taken lightly, and should be left to the experts.

TJ told me a story about Robert Gaté, who was between 65 and 70 at the time, bringing a group of clients down the 'Super Loignan' in Tignes many years ago. The mountainside has many rolls where there is a change of slope, and therefore many potential trigger zones to deal with. As Robert descended he stopped at each critical place to regroup. Then he would either jump on the right spot, or cut the slope, provoking a small slide to control the slope for his clients. He cut four or five slides en route down the mountain, and TJ said it was an amazing lesson in slope control from one of the old local pros.

Plaques à vent, or wind-slab

Wind-transported snow, being ground into very small particles, which binds well to itself but not to other snow layers underneath or to the sides. This forms a plate (plaque) or wind-slab, of varying depth. Plaques can also vary in width, from small (one to two metres) to immense (entire mountain face or bowl). The weight or action of a skier is transmitted throughout the entire plaque to its extremities and can trigger its collapse. The fracture line created may be some distance from where he or she may be skiing or standing.

A contiguous plaque is one that is joined at some point with others and a chain reaction may be triggered by the release of any one of them.

A contiguous plaque, in this sense, is in an area where there are many other plaques. If one releases, it could trigger-off neighbouring plaques at the same time.

The 'run-out' zone.

When choosing a slope to ski you must always be aware of what lies below. The question you must always ask is "if this slope avalanches, where will I end up"?

The ideal slope is a long wide one, which gradually becomes less and less steep towards the bottom. This type of slope would have the perfect 'run-out' zone. If an avalanche occurred the snow would be able to disperse on its way down the mountain, leaving a minimal amount to accumulate at the bottom. If you were caught in a slide on this type of slope, you would have a much better chance of ending up on, or near, the surface.

A slope, which must be avoided at all costs, is one with a hole or embankment at the bottom. In this type of terrain a minimal amount of snow can be fatal. Because there is no 'run-out', instead of dispersing the snow will accumulate in the hole or against the embankment. Caught in even a small slide in this terrain could land you under a couple of metres or more of accumulated snow.

Photo 18, Plate section 2

Several years ago I witnessed two tragic accidents, occurring only three weeks apart, in exactly the same place. The slope in question had never caused a problem but during the previous summer they had widened the piste from the summit of Tovière towards the Arriére Campanules. The re-profiling had dramatically changed the shape of the summit, and therefore the aerodynamics of the wind passing over the ridge. The result was wind-slab building in a place where it had never been a major factor.

In both cases the skiers involved were traversing from one piste to another, no more than 30 metres off the piste and totally unaware of the dangers posed by the hole below them. The slope avalanched while the skiers were traversing and they were swept down into the hole. In both cases the fracture line was only about ten centimetres, which is minimal by avalanche standards, but because there was nowhere for the snow to disperse, it accumulated in the hole and the skiers were later found under three metres of snow. Had these avalanches occurred on a slope with a good 'run-out', the snow would probably have dispersed to a few centimetres and it would have been a scary but beneficial learning experience, instead of a catastrophe.

One accident could be written off as bad luck. But after the second slide occurring within a few weeks, the pisteurs have taken no chances and have bombed that spot after every snowfall (accompanied by wind) ever since.

These were tragic incidents. In both cases the skiers involved were not even trying to ski off-piste; they were simply trying to cut a corner from one piste to another. They were piste skiers who were unequipped and totally unaware. The moment you step foot outside the marked pistes, there are potential hazards and off-piste awareness and procedure must be applied.

Photo 19, Plate section 2

Equally important, when powder skiing, is never to stop above a hole or embankment, especially to regroup or have a picnic.

Another dangerous slope is one with a cliff at the bottom. A very small amount of sliding snow could be enough to carry a skier over the edge. Also be aware of obstacles that you would not want to be swept into. The power of sliding snow is incredible and you would be surprised at how little snow is required to push you along.

(Technically, the 'run-out' zone is the tract where an avalanche starts to slow down, and the area where the snow accumulates is known as the deposition zone. I look at the 'run-out' zone as where the avalanche would flow and where you might end up, such as over a cliff or against an embankment. The deposition zone is included in this description.)

The 'reception zone'.

I first heard this term from my colleague Jean Marc Pic and thought it to be a perfect description. The bottom of what would be the 'run-out' zone in powder conditions becomes the 'reception' zone where there is firm snow on the ground. Now the question you must ask yourself is, "If I fall, and can't stop myself, where will I end up"?

Icy snow, wind-polished snow, and spring snow are all incredible sliding surfaces. And if you fall and can't stop, you will slide all the way to the bottom or until you collide with something along the way. Always choose a fall-line that is obstacle free. Avoid skiing above a crop of rocks, a big tree, a pylon, a cliff, or anything else you would not want to slide over or into. It is scary to watch where some people choose to ski. Sometimes all they need to do is move 10 metres to the left or 15 metres to the right, and instead of skiing a dangerous fall-line they could find a safe obstacle-free fall-line and a more welcoming 'reception' zone.

Beware of the situation above

It is very easy to be drawn to what awaits below on a slope, but it is equally important to be aware of the situation above you as well. And what lies above can give you vital clues as to whether you should ski or traverse a slope or not.

For example, a huge cornice hanging above you indicates a couple of possibilities. Firstly, is there a chance of the cornice dropping off and either landing on you or setting off an avalanche? Cornices do tend to hang around for some time, and under most conditions it would be bad luck for one to fall at the moment you happen to be skiing or traversing underneath it. But on the other hand, you would be pushing your luck to stop underneath a cornice and have a picnic, especially on a hot sunny day. Secondly, and more importantly, a cornice gives you a clue to the direction of prevailing winds. Wind slab develops on the lee side of a slope, which is basically the side underneath the built up cornice. This slope would potentially be loaded up after every windstorm and certainly after every snowfall with even minimal wind. The presence of the cornice tells you that the slope below it could be dangerous because of the distinct possibility of wind slab.

A tragic example of this happened in the spring of 1999. The victim was someone I had known for years. He was at one time a member of the British Freestyle team, and needless to say a very accomplished skier. It was late in the season, when the temperature can rise dramatically during the day, and powder skiing is generally safer in the morning. He was with a group of friends and they had walked up the ridge to ski the North Face of the Foglietta in the neighbouring resort of Ste. Foy. It is a vast and impressive bowl with various steep entrances. It was a hot sunny day, and it was late in the afternoon when he decided to jump off a cornice for a little added excitement. The others had side-slipped in safely and stayed well out of the way.

The last thing he said before jumping was "is everyone beeped up". The shock of his landing set off an avalanche and he was carried away. He and his friends were equipped with beeps and shovels and they managed to locate him very quickly. But unfortunately he was quite deep and digging him out wasn't easy. His friends could not have been quicker, but he died in hospital several days later. Perhaps they were there too late in the day? But chances are if he had realised the implications of the cornice and quietly side-slipped onto the slope like his friends, they would all have made it safely to the bottom.

Another indictor to watch out for would be a gully funnelling down towards you, because gullies are natural flow paths for avalanches. If there were new snow or unstable conditions, the (often unseen) slopes above could release and funnel snow down onto unsuspecting skiers below. Try to avoid being at the bottom of a natural avalanche path, and when it is unavoidable, pass through as quickly as possible.

Skiers and boarders above you could also lead to a dangerous situation and their presence should be noted. If you are about to ski a slope and spot a group of skiers (or boarders) skiing or traversing above you, you must make a decision. Do you feel that the mountain is stable and their presence is not a factor? If they are far enough away do you hurry to ski on towards a safe place and get away from them? If you are in a safe place do you wait until they are no longer a factor? What you choose to do depends on the day and the conditions, but you must be aware of what skiers above are doing and how their presence and behaviour could affect your safety.

There are certain places where a disturbance caused by a single skier can trigger a slide from far above. Often these places give no clues and this is a case where local knowledge comes into its own. Knowing the history of slopes and sectors is invaluable in avoiding dangerous areas that do not give visual clues.

There are many questions to ask about the conditions above. Has the slope avalanched recently or is the entire winter's snowpack sitting above you? Is wind slab a possibility? What will be the effect of other skiers? Assessing the conditions above you can be as important as what lies below, and should enter your thought process before making a decision about where to ski, traverse, or stop.

Regrouping (or Where to Stop)

When off-piste you are living by the 'Golden Rule'. So perhaps the most vulnerable time is when you decide to stop and regroup because the whole party will end up standing together. While skiing and traversing one by one, the group is striving to minimise the stress on the snowpack, but at the moment of regrouping the accumulative weight of the entire party means that the stress will be at a maximum. Because the entire group is exposed and the stress on the snowpack is at a maximum, where you decide to stop and regroup must be chosen with great care.

Photo 20, Plate section 2

Try to choose an 'island' of safety; somewhere that offers some protection. High ground such as a knoll or on top of a ridge is much safer than above an embankment, or in a gully. Being sheltered by a big rock or being amongst some well-established trees is safer than being exposed in the middle of a slope. Sometimes your place of safety may be as subtle as a patch of old denser snow that has been exposed by the wind. You would be safer there than wandering forward into the freshly deposited snow. Look around and analyse the terrain. Ideally, you should decide where you are going to stop before you set off.

Sometimes you need to ski from 'island' to 'island' all the way down the mountain. Your first target may be 50 metres away and the second might be 200 metres further on and so on. Sometimes there may not be a naturally safe place to stop. You may need to ski the entire slope one at a time, waiting for the person in front to finish their run and move to a place of safety before the next skier starts their descent.

Avoid stopping in gullies, as they are a natural path for avalanches. Never stop above holes or embankments because of the lack of a 'run-out'. Be aware of small trees as they are often found in avalanche paths. Small trees are flexible and can bend over under the weight of snow. As soon as they are big enough and lose their life saving flexibility, they will be removed by the flow of snow. Also look for trees that are bent over, they are another clue to natural flow zones. Look instead to shelter yourself in well-established trees. Try to avoid stopping in the middle of big slopes, as there could be a lot of snow above and no protection.

Photo 21, Plate section 2

Animals that live in the alpine environment also use these natural 'islands' of safety. There was an interesting French TV documentary focusing on the behaviour of the Chamois. They actually practice one-by-one traversing between 'islands' led by the dominant female. The herd stops when it feels uneasy approaching a possibly suspect slope, and the Grandmother of the herd leads the way. She will either lead them away if she sees fit, or move on her own to a safe place and then wait for the others to join her. Then she will again lead the herd to another 'island' of safety and so on. The naturalist amusingly opines that this caution stems from evolution—the bold Chamois get avalanched before they get a chance to breed!

Take advantage of the natural safety zones; they can protect you. Study the terrain, and do not expose yourself unnecessarily.

In Summary: Last Day Disaster

This story reflects, and summarises, many of the issues discussed on the preceding pages...

Many times over the years I have seen avalanches from a distance, or have been called to help in a search, and have witnessed the consequences. Unfortunately, all the accidents where I have participated in the rescue have ended tragically.

The scenario is usually fairly similar. The skiers are unequipped. They are often trapped under a lot of snow because of a lack of a run-out zone. And the victims are taken during periods of high avalanche risk. Unfortunately, most of these accidents take place on the most inviting of days. Just after a storm, with beautiful sunny skies. Skiers often feel they have missed out on some skiing during a storm, and when the sun finally comes out, they are only too keen to get in as much as they can.

One such accident took place March 9th 1989. It was late in the afternoon on a beautiful sunny day after a snowfall that had been accompanied by high wind. But, it was a dangerous day with a warning of high avalanche risk and the classic ingredients present*:
1.   An accumulation of fresh snow,
2.   Which had been accompanied by wind, and
3.   Sunny skies promising a rise in temperature.

I was sitting on a terrace on top of the Tête du Solaise sector, enjoying a beer after my afternoon lesson. I looked up toward the front side of the Cugnaï and noticed five skiers traversing across to an untracked powder field. I thought to myself that they were on the wrong slope at the wrong time of day, and kept an interested eye on their progress. I watched them ski down until they dropped behind a ridge and out of my line of sight, and unfortunately I couldn't see them ski all the way to the bottom.

Yes, this point has been repeated at least three times – deliberately so. Along with The Golden Rule, it is imperative that you remember them, if nothing else, once you've put this book down.

I went back to my beer and didn't think any more of it. About a minute later, I looked up and the slope they were skiing avalanched. I had no idea if they were still on the bottom of the slope or not, so I immediately radioed our base station for them to put out the alert. After repeating the message for my colleagues I headed off to help.

As it turned out from studying photos taken by Chris Souillac, the five had finished skiing the slope and had continued on their way. In the meantime, another skier must have seen them skiing powder on his way up the lift, and decided that the snow looked great and it would be a good way to finish his holiday. Near the top of the lift you lose sight of the slope and I'm sure the skier didn't see the avalanche occur. After arriving at the summit, he skied around the corner and traversed next to the avalanche, and started skiing down. After a few turns he set off another plaque and was swept 200 metres down the mountain.

The pisteurs (ski patrol) probably witnessed the first slide from a manned piste hut and were already in motion. I was responding to the first avalanche and was oblivious to the fact that a second slide had occurred. I was on my way but needed to take a drag-lift followed by a 15 to 18 minute chairlift. By the time I arrived about 25 minutes had passed and a few pisteurs were already there trying in vain to locate a signal with their beeps. Several minutes later a couple more pisteurs arrived on the back of a piste machine loaded up with probes and shovels. Coco (the head pisteur of the Solaise sector at the time) immediately set up a line and organised a probe search. Because we only numbered 15 or so, the area covered by the search would not be very wide and it would be critical to start the search in the right place. While the others had been checking for a signal, Coco had been studying the flow of the avalanche and knew exactly where he wanted to begin.

Coco had chosen his spot perfectly. Miraculously, the woman next to me touched the victim with her very first probe. Unfortunately, there was an embankment and the victim was under two-plus metres of snow. Even with big snow shovels it took a further 15 to 20 furious minutes to uncover the victim's blue face. Three or four of the volunteers were doctors, and they immediately administered mouth-to-mouth and cardiac massage. A

Probe Search

Probes are about five metres long and are made of metal. In a probe search you stand shoulder to shoulder with the person next to you, and you push the probe all the way down to the bottom. You then must decide whether you are touching the ground, a rock, or a body. If you can not reach the bottom you must signal and the spot will be marked and later rechecked. When everyone has probed their spot, the search leader will signal for the entire line to move forward a foot and everyone probes again. You must probe every square foot to guarantee a thorough search and it can be very time consuming, and because of the weight and height of the probes, is incredibly tiring.

See Photo 22, Plate section 2

few minutes later the rescue helicopter from Courchevel arrived with paramedics and medical equipment. Unfortunately the mouth-to-mouth and heart massage were having no effect, so they injected adrenalin straight into the victim's heart.

Sadly he didn't survive. The lift pass around his neck showed that it was the last day of his holiday, and apparently his tour bus had been waiting at the bottom while he pushed his luck and took one last run.

Photo 23, Plate section 2

Much went on that particular day, and there were many lessons to be learned from that tragic accident. Some of the lessons summarise much of what we have already covered. First off, the three big and obvious factors were present. Regardless of the state of the underlying layers in the snowpack, anytime you have an accumulation of **fresh snow**, accompanied by **wind**, and then a **rise in temperature**, there will be an increase in avalanche risk. The heavier the snowfall, the stronger the wind, and the warmer it gets the following day, the more dramatic the increase in risk will be. These are obvious signs that any aware skier can keep track of.

Besides the resort's warnings of high avalanche risk and the three main factors present, there were very obvious **visual clues** to instability as well. The slope which the victim attempted to ski had already slid in five or six different places during the day. You could look across the face, from one end to the other, perhaps 300 metres away, and see the various areas where 'plaques' had popped out. This alone is enough of a warning. But these 'plaques' had no signs of tracks leading into them, which meant they released naturally, without the added weight of a skier or skiers. When the mountain is letting go naturally, the risk doesn't get much higher.

This accident also emphasises the importance of being **equipped and prepared** within the group to deal with an avalanche. You must act immediately and efficiently to have any realistic chance of locating and digging out a victim within the fifteen minute target. And there just is no time to rely on help from the security services. This avalanche took place within sight of a manned piste station and the alert could not have been quicker. The rescue services were *en route* to the accident within seconds (and probably in advance of the second slide) but it still took valuable minutes for the first pisteurs to arrive on the scene.

It took 25 minutes or so to equip and organise a probe search. So, I estimate that from the avalanche to the uncovering of the victim's face took around 45 minutes and it would have been physically impossible to have located him and dug him out any sooner. Had the victim been wearing a **beep** the pisteurs could have located him immediately instead of waiting for the probes and volunteers to arrive. Even when in sight of a manned piste station it can take too long for the rescue services to be successful if the victim is not wearing a beep, and many accidents off-piste can go for hours before being reported. Again, you must be prepared to mount your own search and rescue, as help from the outside cannot be relied on.

This particular avalanche occurred on a slope with a **poor run-out zone**. There was a slight embankment at the bottom and the snow accumulated to between three and four metres. The victim was found under two-plus metres of snow and did not have much of a chance. It was a big slide, but had there been a better run-out zone the victim would have had a much better chance of staying near the surface. There is a major difference between being 50 centimetres to a metre under the snow, compared to over two metres, and the shape of the run-out zone can make the difference. Always be aware of potential terrain traps below you.

The importance of **radio or telephone contact** to the outside world also springs to mind. At the time of this avalanche Val d'Isère shared a helicopter with Courchevel, but now each resort has its own rescue helicopter. If you are in need of assistance and can contact the rescue services directly, help can be at hand very quickly. You may be able to locate and dig out a victim quickly but it may be the speed at which the victim gets to a hospital that makes the difference between surviving or not. If you are out in the backcountry and someone is injured and couldn't continue, radio contact can also make a quicker and a less painful and complicated evacuation possible. Contact with the rescue services can be a life saving asset and should never be underestimated.

Off-piste skiing is a team sport and it is very unwise to ski off-piste alone. If anything happens you could be stranded and in serious trouble. This avalanche victim was **skiing on his own** and if he had been out of sight of the lifts and pisteurs' station, it could have been hours or perhaps days before someone might have realised what had happened to him. When someone goes missing in a resort there will be a search. Pisteurs, instructors, and volunteers are involved and, as you can imagine, it can be very time consuming and potentially dangerous for the rescue team. These situations are minimised if people are skiing with friends who know where they are, or at least, where they might be.

It was a tragic and unnecessary accident. It was an obviously dangerous day and so many of the basic rules and signs were ignored, but the outcome was predictable. He was the first dead person I have ever seen, and, unfortunately, he wasn't the last.

Chapter Five

More Food for Thought

HERE ARE a few extra tips to help keep you out of trouble...

Avoid kick-turns on steep slopes

As a general rule, I ask my clients to avoid doing kick-turns on steep slopes when there are firm snow conditions. Firstly, most people cannot comfortably and consistently complete them. Secondly, the consequences of a missed kick-turn can be terrifying.

When someone blows a kick-turn they have one leg pointing east, one leg pointing west, and they are stuck in the middle trying to do their best. They then fall headfirst down the mountain and are off to the races. Sliding headfirst with each leg pointing in a different direction is an incredibly awkward position and makes it next to impossible to execute the self-arrest. From this position a skier would slide all the way to the bottom, or until they collide headfirst with something along the way.

In deep snow I don't worry too much about it and as long as we are in a safe place allow people to practice kick-turns if they wish. A blown kick-turn in powder doesn't really matter because the skier will not slide anywhere. But beware, if you are stiff and lack flexibility, kick-turns can be a good way to injure yourself.

I have a very eccentric client named Kevin, who would never dream of doing a kick-turn on a steep slope after his last attempt. It was several years ago in April and I decided to take the group to La Rosière/La Thuile for a day trip. It is a great day out with excellent spring snow on the French side in the morning, followed by a ski into Italy for a fabulous pasta lunch, then a gentle ski back to the French side in the afternoon. All in all, a very pleasant and normally, a stress-free excursion.

We had skied several runs of excellent spring snow and I was working our way around a bowl, following the sun so that we could ski the slopes at that moment when the surface layer had softened "à point", as the French would say. The slope had various changes where it would gradually roll off, and you could not see below without skiing up to the change of slope and looking. I skied down to a roll-off and stopped so that the others would have room to turn around if necessary. I waited for them to regroup before moving forward and peering down the next slope.

I did not like the look of the fall-line directly below me. There were a few nasty little rocks sticking three or four inches out of the snow. The rocks were not very big but had a sharp and jagged look to them, and could easily make a mess out of anyone who slid over them. I inspected the terrain in both directions and 20 metres to my right lay the obvious choice, an obstacle free fall-line with clean untracked snow.

The group was a few metres above me and most of them were pointing in the right direction. Kevin was grinning from ear to ear, as usual, but he was unfortunately pointing the other way. I told the group that we were going to the right, explained why, and said, " no kick-turns, do a little stem turn but absolutely no kick-turns please". I then looked Kevin straight in the eye (we were both wearing sunglasses but I could tell we had eye to eye contact) and said directly to him, "Kev, no kick-turns". He nodded his head rapidly like an eager puppy, acknowledging that he had heard me and obviously keen to get back to the spring snow. Because he was one metre above me, I side-slipped back out of his way so he could get turned around.

No sooner had I turned my back and Kevin was stuck half way through a kick-turn, and was teetering back and forth before pitching himself head first down the slope. He instantly accelerated and slid 50 metres between the rocks, with his arms covering his head for protection, to the bottom, and fortunately, a welcoming reception zone. We all let out a huge sigh of relief when he stood up in one piece, grinned, and waved back up towards us. How Kevin was spared the wrath of the tooth-like rocks no one will ever know.

We all made our way (the others decided they preferred my route) to the bottom and dusted him off. I then asked his girlfriend Jane what she thought about his little blunder. She just stared at him and said, "Kevin, you ass—".

I decided that that was enough excitement for one morning, so we skied over the Col to Italy and down towards the restaurant. The Italian side was immaculately groomed and the pistes were empty, so I thought it was the perfect opportunity for a good piste cruise before lunch. I took off at the top and at well spaced intervals, my clients followed. I skied close to a kilometre and decided to stop and regroup.

One by one they arrived except for Kevin and Pete (who was bringing up the rear with an extra radio). A minute later Pete radioed down to say that Kevin has had a minor explosion, that he is fine but his equipment is spread out all over the piste, and that they will collect it and rejoin us shortly. Jane groaned "ohh Keeviin". Five seconds later Pete chuckled into his radio, "Hey Wayne! I think we better get this guy to a bar". Thanks to Kevin, we had a long leisurely lunch and plenty to talk about.

Ski with a friend

Off-piste skiing is a team sport where you work together with other skiers in the group to minimise the risks and protect yourselves. If anything goes wrong you have immediate support to help deal with any emergency that might arise. The more extreme the skiing, the less people you want involved - but one is not an option.

If you are alone in the mountains and hurt, or taken in an avalanche, the consequences could be extreme. If injured there would be no one to help make you as comfortable as possible, or to go in search of assistance. If taken and buried by an avalanche, unless someone had witnessed it from a distance and could raise an alarm, you would die there and no one would know.

There is a very eccentric local Frenchman named Olivier who always skis alone. I often see him at the bottom on the day's first lift, equipped with two ice axes, ropes, and I can only guess at what else. I have never actually seen him skiing and can only imagine where he goes and what he gets up to, but it is obvious that he takes his skiing very seriously. One morning I saw him with a crash helmet and two huge, red, homemade wings that he had built. His plan was to shuss a steep couloir and use his wings as stabilisers. (Tens years later I can still vividly picture the sight of him that morning). I'm not sure whether he tells someone where he is skiing each day or not, but he is fully aware of the risks he is taking and chooses to spend his time in the mountains on his own. Because Olivier is (I think) of sound mind, I respect his decision and when seeing him I always smile to myself and wonder where is he going. But I must stress that the solo act is not the recommended way of travelling in the mountains.

Ski pole straps - to use or not to use?

There is a time when you should use your pole straps and there is a time when you should definitely take them off. I personally never ski with my straps attached, on or off-piste, but feel it can be especially important in deep snow. The last thing you would want is to be dragged under in an avalanche because of your poles. If strapless and taken in a slide, you could release your poles and free your arms to do whatever it takes to save yourself, whether it be swim, grab for a tree, or perhaps try to create an air pocket. Being strapless could also help save you from being twisted or pinned in an awkward position.

Another situation for strapless skiing would be in the trees. You would not want to catch a basket on a branch or stump and damage your thumb, wrist, elbow, or shoulder because you are attached to the pole. Even on piste there are many thumb injuries occurring because of the use of pole straps. Without pole straps you can simply let go when you feel a potentially damaging jerk or throw them away if taken in a slide.

Unfortunately there are drawbacks to this theory. If skiers are unaccustomed to this practice, I find that they let go of their poles just about every time they fall over in deep snow. The last thing you need is to search around for ski poles in the middle of the slope in powder snow. It defeats the purpose of safety to spend extra time exposed on a slope because of a lost ski pole and it can be incredibly time consuming. If skiers cannot hang onto their poles when they fall, I tell them to forget it and put their straps back on. The only other time I would tell skiers to put their straps on is when traversing on spring snow. If I feel that the conditions are stable, the problem becomes someone dropping a pole and having it slide to the bottom. This is fine if you are about to ski down, but if you need to remain high on a traverse, a dropped pole can seriously alter your plans.

I think it is worth practising without your pole straps on the piste. It doesn't take long to get use to hanging on to them when you fall, and it could make a difference off-piste. Conversely, if you enjoy a high-speed piste cruise from time to time, a fall at speed is another good time to free yourself of your poles.

Following Tracks

Following tracks is not a good idea. You might get lucky and be led into wonderful snow and perfect terrain, or you might find yourself in a situation you will regret. By following tracks you could easily put yourself in danger, seriously annoy the people you are following or, much worse, endanger them as well.

Skiers follow tracks for various reasons. It is very tempting for people who are unsure of where they are to follow tracks. Some skiers are just inquisitive and others do not want to miss out on the possibility of greener, more exciting pastures. They all feel that someone who knew exactly where he or she was going made the tracks, and that it must be safe. Unfortunately, nothing could be further from the truth.

There is nothing to guarantee that someone who knows the area has made the tracks you are following, or that they are a good judge of whether the conditions are stable or not. They could very easily be leading you into hazardous conditions. Or they could be very experienced skiers en route to some very challenging skiing - a slope that they can technically handle, but one that may be way above your own skiing level. By following tracks you could easily endanger yourself by landing in terrain that is far beyond your capabilities.

Another possibility is that you could be following a group of experienced off-piste skiers who have waited a long time for just the right conditions to ski a certain slope. The right conditions however, might not include an extra person or persons, cutting back and forth above them or adding extra weight to the snowpack. Following behind them could change their position from one of being relaxed and in control, to stressed and praying that you do not make a mistake which could jeopardise their safety.

Many skiers also mistakenly believe that once a slope has been skied it must be safe. Tracks on a slope do not necessarily mean that the slope is safe to ski, and it can be the fiftieth skier down that triggers an avalanche. They had a situation heli-skiing in Canada a few years ago where they must have had fifty or more tracks on the same mountainside. At the end of the day when all the skiers were safely back at the lodge, the entire slope buckled. It didn't quite slide but had fracture lines all through it, and they must have been amazed and probably felt lucky that it hadn't slid during the day while being skied (There is a photo of the slope in Tony Daffern's *Avalanche Safety for Skiers & Climbers*). In Fred Foxon's avalanche, he was the seventh skier down the couloir. Remember that tracks do not necessarily equate to safety.

Once to look, twice to cook!

I've unfortunately learned the hard way over the years about behaving badly in unfamiliar terrain. If you are unsure about what lies around the corner or over the brow, do not throw yourself into it, or over it, at breakneck speed. This might sound obvious but you would be surprised at how many people hurt themselves by not skiing cautiously and using common sense in unfamiliar territory.

My first lesson came at the tender age of thirteen. At this stage my brother Dennis and I were into jumping, and one of our favourite launch pads was known as 'springboard'. We skied each weekend at Lake Louise and knew our terrain like the back of our hands. But, in-between visits, the mountain had five or six days for the conditions to change.

The previous weekend we had both jumped 'springboard' several times, landing on the steep but smooth slope on the other side of take-off. We returned with our friend Webby the following Saturday morning raring to go. Unfortunately, I went first. I pushed off and skied towards the lip of the jump, trying to judge my speed so that I wouldn't fly into orbit. I hit the take-off and leapt into the air. But a split-second later I knew I was in serious trouble. Since our last visit the perfectly smooth landing had been transformed into a mogul field. I was madly wind-milling my arms around at great speed hoping to remain airborne a little longer, trying desperately to postpone the inevitable. My flight came to an abrupt end as I came crashing back down to earth with a sickening thud. I seemed to blow up, and my poles disappeared along with my hat and goggles. Snow was flying everywhere and I remember closing my eyes to it all, trying to block it out. I suddenly realized that I was accelerating downhill through the bump field, but sliding wasn't the only problem on my mind.

In those days the skis were attached to the boots by leather safety straps (anything but safe), and after the fall you were more worried about being beaten to a pulp by your flailing skis then you ever were about sliding into something. So I was protecting my head with both hands and elbows when I hit the tree. I was lying horizontally across the slope, facing uphill at the moment of impact. I took the tree in the small of the back, and my head and feet almost met behind me as I was contorted into a backward U-shape. I had never come to such an abrupt stop in all my life. My breath exploded from my lungs, and breathing was impossible. I was frozen with fear because I couldn't feel anything and I remembered hearing a loud 'crack'. My brother and Webby came down and Dennis cried, "Where the hell is he?" A couple of seconds later Webby yelled, "Holy cow, he's in the goddam tree."

It turned out that the loud 'crack' was the branches breaking as they (thankfully) slowed my momentum before slamming into the trunk of the tree. I ended up very bruised and 'just' chipped a vertebra. I was also very lucky. It was the last time any of us ever took another jump without first surveying the landing.

Lesson number two came many years later during my second season in Val d'Isère. It was early May and my friends and I were skiing superb spring snow at Le Fornet. We were a little way off our regular route so we didn't intimately know the terrain. Being close to twenty years younger, we habitually skied much faster in those days. The snow was unmarked, conducive to high-speed GS turns, and we were really letting it go. Unfortunately on this day, I also remember trying to show off for this beautiful girl who had joined us.

My friends had skied off first and I had stayed behind to chat up the girl, and ended up kissing her. Then with my head in the clouds and dizzy with desire, I pushed off and headed down towards my companions, skiing way too quickly and desperate to impress. My friends were looming in front of me and I took a little air and, at about a half-metre off the ground, followed the contour of the slope for about 15 to 20 metres. Suddenly, at the end of my flight path was an unavoidable embankment. The others were grouped together with ringside seats to the event that was about to happen. Francis, who was a bit of a card, turned to the others and said, "Wow, this is going to be messy."

I piled into the embankment face first, then my feet kipped over my head and the cart-wheeling began. My face hit, then my feet, face, feet, face, feet, face, feet. All I could see was white, blue, white, blue, white, blue. It seemed to go on forever. It was incredibly violent and I kept waiting for my back to break, thinking that I was going to be in a wheelchair for the rest of my life. Finally, I came to a stop but was afraid to move.

I could hear the others taking in a huge collective breath when Francis said, "I think he's dead." I wiggled my toes and realized I hadn't done the damage I deserved. My friend Stretch (he was 6' 3" when he was 12 and never grew another inch) who had seen his father killed in an industrial explosion, skied up to me with tears running down his cheeks and said, "I have never seen anything like that except when my Dad was killed. It was like you were a rag doll and I just threw you across a room".

It took fifteen minutes or so to pull myself back together. When we were just about to ski away, Francis asked about my sunglasses that had left my face long ago. We climbed back up and found them right where I had left them. Implanted two-feet deep in the embankment where my face had first hit.

That was the end of my season. My face swelled up like a balloon, and my neck and back were stiff and sore. And to add insult to injury, I never got the girl.

Skiing under control in unfamiliar territory is crucial. And because of changing conditions, even terrain that you know intimately can hold some nasty surprises. I was very lucky on both these occasions, and sometimes wonder how I survived my misspent youth.

My friend Russell used to love to take out his 223cm downhill skis for a cruise about once a week, and he had some very good and sensible advice. When skiing quickly he would always scout out the terrain before putting the foot down, and he always said, "Once to look, twice to cook!" Free-riders, take note.

Chapter Six

Teamwork

IF 'THE GOLDEN RULE' is the core of off-piste procedure, then teamwork is the backbone. Good off-piste habits begin with teamwork and every procedure must be co-ordinated as a team. It only takes one person to make a mistake at the wrong time to endanger someone else, possibly the whole party, or others you may be sharing the mountain with. But to work successfully as a team each member must know what is expected of them, and here are some of the procedures I stress.

Skiing one at a time

Besides respecting the 'Golden Rule', skiing one at a time has other benefits. Having only one skier on the slope ensures that your group will keep the stress on the snowpack to the absolute minimum. One skier weighs less than two, two less than three, and so on. And it is not only a question of body weight, but also the magnified stresses caused by the force of the turns, and the stress of one skier's turns is much less than the combined stresses of multiple skiers.

Photo 24, Plate section 2.

Having one skier on the slope also gives each skier a chance to have the slope to themselves, and to enjoy it without being pressed from behind by someone else. It is much more relaxing and rewarding to have an open slope before you without pressure from someone you are skiing with. At times you may feel pressured by other groups of skiers, and the last thing you need is to create stress within your own party.

Some slopes and conditions call for skiing an entire slope one by one, with each skier waiting patiently for the person before them to ski to the bottom and move off to a place of safety before setting off. Other slopes and different conditions may not need such strict discipline. In a situation where the slope is very gentle and there is no danger from above, I might have my group leave 35 metres between skiers to keep the group moving, yet still leave enough space for everyone to feel relaxed and unhurried. Except in these gentle conditions I habitually ski one by one so that my clients are developing good off-piste habits, but it is up to the group members to execute whatever you are trying to achieve.

Traversing

The goal when traversing is to stay far enough apart so that if anything ever goes wrong, you are in a 'six searching for one' situation, not the other way around. But how far apart is far enough? Conditions change and some slopes are safer to cross than others so a safe distance between skiers will vary. A slope in spring conditions may be safe to traverse with 20 metres between skiers and the same slope in mid-winter, with 40 centimetres of fresh snow, may call for a spacing of 150 metres or more.

Photo 25, Plate section 2.

Once a distance between skiers has been decided upon, it is up to the individuals in the group to maintain that spacing. In fresh snow this can be easier said than done and requires good concentration. When making a traverse in deep snow, the traverse will become quicker with each skier who uses it. An inexperienced group will find themselves catching up with one another and eventually could end up all bunched together. An avalanche now would be a disaster, taking the entire party. This situation does happen and can be avoided.

An experienced team in the same situation would know from past traverses that the track would quicken, and they would allow more time from skier to skier before starting off. If they felt they were catching up with the skier in front, they would slow down or stop. The person behind seeing someone slowing down or stopping would do the same, and so on.

To build good traverse habits I spread the group out even when I know it is perfectly safe, so that good spacing, and maintaining that spacing, becomes the norm. Teamwork again is the key.

Protect the weakest skier

It is always important to ski to the limitations of the weakest skier. A chain is only as strong as its weakest link, and an off-piste team is the same. If you are on a steep slope with firm snow, and the entire party is comfortable and competent except for one, that one skier is being put under enormous pressure. If they were to fall and slide, they could be in a life-threatening situation.

Another example would be in deep snow with a question over the snowpack's stability. Someone who is skiing smoothly and linking turns in the fall-line, is stressing the snow much less than a falling skier or one who makes a turn or two and then shoots off across the mountain. The impact of the body with each fall is a potential 'trigger' for an avalanche, as is the 'cutting' of the slope when a skier leaves the fall-line. In these cases the weakest skier is not only endangering themselves, but also the people they are skiing with. These are extreme examples, but pushing a skier past his or her limits is a dangerous game and can have serious consequences.

If one does not have the patience to wait for the slowest skier, or the sense to choose terrain that suits them, the weaker skier should not be skiing in that group. This applies to piste skiing as much as it does to off-piste. More often than not, the less experienced skier is terrified and has a horrible time, and the unlucky ones end up injuring themselves. You see it time and time again when friends who are better skiers try, with perfectly good intentions, to include friends who are just not up to it and it usually ends in tears. Be very patient and attentive when taking a less experienced skier along, and be very careful about who you choose to ski with.

Another rule of thumb is to never leave the weakest to bring up the rear, and this is especially important if there is a noticeable difference in levels within the group. This will save time, and avoid potentially dangerous situations. For example, if you left the weakest skier to go last on a long slope with 30 centimetres of powder and they fell and lost a ski or injured themselves, there would be no one above to come down and help. The last thing you need is someone hurt or struggling to find a ski in deep snow, and you could end up needing to walk back up the mountain in knee-deep snow to help.

Leaving the weakest behind can also put them under pressure, and some circumstances do not need added pressure thrown into the equation. I know that some skiers feel much more confident knowing there is someone they trust behind them in case they get stuck. It is up to the group members to be looking out for one another and taking turns to bring up the near to protect and encourage the weakest.

Keep an eye on the sweeper

It is important to survey the progress of the last skier in the group. Because he or she is bringing up the rear, if anything goes wrong there is no one to help them from above. Any help will come from below, which means a time-consuming climb back uphill. You should always try to have the person in front or behind in sight, but there are situations when you may lose visual contact momentarily. Because you may be spread out across the mountain, it is up to the penultimate skier to make sure that the last party member is safe.

I had a situation several years ago when the most experienced member of the team, who was bringing up the rear, had a potentially serious problem. We had been skiing 25 to 30 centimetres of powder in the Arselle sector and had skied our way to the bottom. After regrouping we spread out about 50 metres apart for the traverse back to the chairlift and I cut the trail out. I made a shallow traverse so that it would not become too quick for the last skiers in the group, and stopped when we arrived back at the piste. Because of the contour of the terrain it was impossible to see the last couple of skiers in the party, and we waited while, one by one, the others joined us. But my friend Rob, who was at the back of the group, did not appear when he should have. I had a bad feeling about it and started walking back uphill along the traverse hoping to get a glimpse of him. I came over a knoll and had a clear view for several hundred metres, and still could not see Rob. I was now starting to worry, as he should have been in sight.

During the traverse we had crossed a little gully, about two metres across and a couple of metres deep. When Rob had skied across the gully the snow-bridge had collapsed and he had fallen headfirst and was trapped. I was wondering what could have happened to him as I climbed back uphill, and suddenly remembered the little ravine.

After five minutes or so I came to the gully and found Rob upside down. He had tipped over headfirst and the tips and tails of his skis were caught on either side of the dip. Rob was hanging head down with his feet still in his bindings, in an incredibly awkward position, and his arms were pinned so that he could hardly move them. He had hit his face while falling and his goggles had cut him, resulting in blood running into his right eye. Thankfully his face was clear of snow and besides being terribly uncomfortable he was able to breathe normally. But, he had spent five uneasy minutes or longer, bleeding, with the blood rushing to his head, and wondering if help was on its way. Rob was incredibly relieved to finally have someone arrive to free him from his bindings and his entrapment.

It would have been easy to continue on to the lift after reaching the piste, but because the last couple of skiers were not within sight, we had stopped and waited. Rob could have hit his head or have had his face covered in snow, and because no one was behind him, his only chance of help was from below. Keep the last skier in sight and if you are leading people, do not distance yourself too far from the people behind you. The further you go the longer and more time consuming the climb back uphill.

Eliminate selfish behaviour

One sure way to ruin the good atmosphere in a group is selfish behaviour. There is no room for selfishness as it causes stress, which could lead to a dangerous situation. Stressed people make mistakes, and mistakes are what we are striving to avoid off-piste.

One of the most easily noted forms of selfishness within a group is the individual who always jumps in first after the guide. Most teams take it in turn having 'next tracks' after the guide, following them on the piste, and bringing up the rear. The fastest way to alienate yourself from the others you are skiing with is to persistently hang around at the front of the group.

Another sure way of causing stress is to be impatient. Some people just can't seem to wait their turn when it comes to traversing or skiing, and follow the skier in front too closely. Besides potentially overloading the snowpack, pressure from behind takes away from the enjoyment of the skier who should have an unimpeded run. Following too closely is also a recipe for a collision, which should never happen within a group.

But perhaps the most dangerous form of selfishness comes from the type who tries to pressure the guide into doing more than he or she has chosen to do.

Professionals have a desire to do their utmost to please their clients. They want to show their clients great skiing, and stretch them a little while showing them new horizons. Off-piste guides often put pressure on themselves because of their will to satisfy their followers, and there is a fine line that does not need to be crossed. Your guide will be doing his or her best to show you a great time, and more importantly, keep you safe. They will have a reason for every decision they make regarding snow and terrain. Do yourself, the others in the group and your guide a favour. Respect your guide's decisions and refrain from pushing for more than they are comfortable to do.

See Photo 26, Plate section 2 – and contrast it with Photo 27.

Selfishness has no place in the mountains. One person can ruin five other people's holiday and perhaps put them in danger along the way. I give people a chance, but if they continue to show a selfish tendency, I refuse to ski with them. Selfish behaviour detracts from the enjoyment and spirit of the group - which is completely unnecessary on a long awaited holiday - and selfishness can endanger others, which is totally unacceptable in the mountains.

Teamwork is vital for safe skiing and each team member has a part to play, from the weakest in the group to the strongest. Sometimes the weakest skier may be the strongest on a climb and be able to carry extra gear, and the strongest skier may suffer from vertigo and need support on the steeper slopes. The strongest skier may need to show some patience, and be willing to forfeit some personal pleasure to be there for someone who may need assistance. The weakest skier should do everything possible to not hold up the group, such as getting up and dusting themselves off as quickly as possible after a fall. Usually the most comfortable place to be in the group is somewhere in the middle. It helps everyone's understanding of teamwork to have experienced for themselves, at some point, being the weakest in the group, the strongest, and somewhere in the middle.

Working for and with one-another builds a great ambience within the group and helps avoid tricky situations. I think recognising that there are potential risks off-piste as individuals and as a group, and then trusting one another within the group to play their part towards the goal of minimizing the risks, builds an incredible camaraderie within the team. It is very satisfying and the reason off-piste skiing is a sport that makes and (I know it sounds corny) then bonds friendships. There are not many situations in life where adults will trust their lives to someone else's behaviour, but off-piste skiing is one of them.

Choose your friends carefully

If you decide not to ski with a professional, make sure you choose your friends carefully. Skiers who are accustomed to skiing for themselves usually do not understand the needs of less experienced skiers. Choice of terrain, choice of snow, evaluation of risks, and the assessment of your ability are very important decisions, and a huge responsibility. Do you really want these decisions being made by a friend who has just spent several holidays or a season or two in a resort?

I had a client in February during the big snow period of the 1998-99 season who had never spent any real time off-piste before. He was with a couple of friends who were more experienced skiers but they were patient and wanted to baptise him to the joys of deep snow skiing, so we all skied together at a slower pace. It was some of the best snow that we'd had in years, but because of the problems in Austria and the fact that the press had blown things way out of proportion, many skiers were staying away. It turned out that they were the only clients I had that week.

Everything worked out well because it was a delicate time and having a small group in these conditions was advantageous, and John was protected by his friends and my girlfriend, who were all experienced off-piste skiers. He caught on very quickly and we made a very good team. John would stay in the middle of the group and his confidence was growing rapidly. There had been plenty of snow and the avalanche risk was high, but there was superb skiing on gentle terrain, to the side of the pistes, and on the pistes themselves. We were skiing deep powder and I was confident that we weren't taking any unnecessary risks. After three mornings of wonderful conditions, John was skiing very well, looked confident, and was really pleased with himself.

But on the morning of the fourth day, John was falling all over the place and didn't seem at all comfortable. I asked him what was wrong and he told me about the nightmare he had experienced the previous afternoon. He had a cousin who was spending the winter in town and he had invited him skiing after our morning session. It was a hot afternoon, the avalanche risk was high and increasing, and his cousin had taken him off-piste. Not only had he taken him off-piste but also he had taken him to the Banane, which is an area that must be treated very carefully at the best of times, but late in the afternoon after 30 centimetres of fresh snow? I couldn't imagine a worse place to be that particular afternoon, and was furious that his cousin could be so irresponsible. I was upset that he had put John in danger and of the effect that it had had on John's skiing and confidence. One afternoon of reckless behaviour undid much of three days patient work.

We took a couple of steps back and slowly went about the task of rebuilding John's confidence. He had been skiing well and enjoying himself, so he thankfully made a fairly quick recovery. Fortunately, the only thing he suffered from his inappropriate afternoon off-piste was a short-lived confidence crisis.

Choose your friends carefully. They will be anxious to show you a good time and to share their environment with you. They may have the best intentions in the world, but chances are they will not be experienced in the delicacies of the needs and goals of the less experienced. And the fact that they seem to know their way around does not necessarily make them a good judge of what is safe, and more importantly, what isn't.

For Male Eyes Only

The typical French male firmly believes that because they have been born with the technology, it is their right to take full advantage of it. They will happily relieve themselves whenever and wherever the urge comes over them. North Americans, and some Brits, may find this lack of privacy uncomfortable, or perhaps even repulsive. But I say, "When in Rome, do like the French."

Now, when arriving on a wonderful powder slope or perfect spring pitch, the adrenalin is usually pumping. I find it difficult to concentrate and enjoy my skiing to the fullest with a full bladder, and when excited the urge becomes even stronger. I have to admit to usually taking a pee before opening a big slope. But, I do have a few words of advice. No matter how perfect the snow, no matter how intoxicated you may be about the slope to be skied, take a few extra seconds and make sure you have correctly tucked yourself away before yanking up on your zip.

Many years ago I was skiing with my friend Rob when we both decided it was time to stop and relieve ourselves. We pulled over about a hundred metres from the piste to do the business. It was a beautiful day and we where admiring the scenery and saying something typical like, "God, nothing in the world feels better than this". Two seconds later I let out a hair-raising scream as I had pulled up a millisecond early on my zipper.

I looked down and couldn't believe what I'd done. There was way too much skin caught between the teeth of my fly. I said, " Rob, we have a problem". Rob immediately responded with, "What do you mean – we?" I whimpered, "That's not funny Rob. I think I need some help". Rob, being a true friend, shuffled up and bent over to get a bird's eye view of the situation. All he could say was, "Shit, you poor bastard". I was in pain and really quite fearful about what needed to be done next, and knew there was absolutely no way that I was going to be able to yank the zipper myself. I pleaded to Rob, "Please Rob, I think I'm going to need a hand". Rob bravely bent over and grabbed my dick in one hand, and my zip in the other, and said, "It's your call. Up, or down."

By this stage I was close to panicking. What the people on the lift one hundred metres away must of thought I have no idea. All they could see were two males, standing side by side, with one bending over and handling the other's organ. I was in shock and totally confused, "Up, no down, up, down, no, just a second."

After a couple of seconds thought, the realisation that down was the only way to go came over both of us at the same moment. Rob gave an almighty tug down on my zip and I responded with an almighty scream.

The relief was incredible. I was puffing away trying to regain my breath, with eyes watering, when Rob said, "Friendship is one thing, but you owe me one buddy". I replied with, "Please Rob, don't ever get that thing of yours caught".

I was so shaken by the experience that I searched out trousers with button flies for years afterwards and, still to this day, take my time when preparing to do up my fly. So, no matter how inviting that powder might be, do yourself and your friends a favour. Be patient, slow down, and make sure you tuck yourself in properly. Speaking of choosing your friends carefully....

Chapter Seven

Mountain Etiquette

WHEN I FIRST arrived in Val d'Isère, some 20 years ago, you could easily find fresh snow for weeks after a snowfall. In the springtime, the entire resort had perfect, billiard-table smooth, spring snow. Untracked snow seemed to be the norm and you didn't need to look too hard to find it. You could ski off-piste without seeing many other skiers, and when you did you would usually wave a friendly greeting to a fellow enthusiast. If they were in front of you, you would patiently wait and let them finish their run and move off a safe distance before you continued your descent. This was the safe and stress-free way of doing things.

Today it is a totally different story. There are so many more people skiing off-piste, and some resorts now become tracked-out in a single morning. Everyone wants to ski powder, and they don't care how they get it. I call it 'powder frenzy' and relate this crazed behaviour to that of the sharks 'feeding frenzy'. People push and shove, and behave with a total lack of respect towards everyone else on the mountain. This comportment is dangerous, stressful, and totally destroys the ambience and enjoyment of being in the mountains.

An example of this behaviour can be seen in Photo 27, Plate section 2.

Skiers also make little or no effort to conserve the quality of the snow. Powder snow is needlessly wasted and, in the spring, wonderful slopes are ruined in one day by skiers who are unaware, or uncaring, of 'snow management'.

You can still spend much of your time off-piste alone with your group, but it is a fact that there will be times when you must share the mountain with others. How you behave will either minimise risk and stress, or create it. Off-piste etiquette has a vital role to play in keeping you in a safe and enjoyable environment, and snow management can make the difference between wonderful and un-skiable conditions.

Etiquette and snow management (covered in next section) go hand in hand. Here are some of the ground rules that should be standard procedure...

Waiting for skiers below

One of the dangers in powder skiing is that of having an avalanche 'cut' down on top of you by unaware skiers above. This happens every season and there have even been cases of powder crazed skiers cutting avalanches down onto children on the pistes. You can do your best to control what lies in front of you, but you are at the mercy of skiers above you. This can be extremely annoying and frustrating and made all the worse when you know that they followed you in the first place.

When *you* arrive above a group of skiers below, you should stop and wait. Let them finish their run and either move to an 'island' of safety or a safe distance away. This allows the group below to enjoy a safer run because you have done the polite thing. If the skiers below are aware of the what-and-why's of your actions, they will probably wave a 'thank you' in acknowledgement.

Another situation that can arise is when someone skiing in your group falls. It is important to wait for the skier to get up and move on before skiing down. If someone is down and you start a slide, they are trapped and have no chance of escape. The only time you would come down on top of a fallen skier would be to help look for a lost ski, or if the skier was injured.

Who gets first tracks?

When powder skiing there is often a need for cutting or making a track in soft snow across to the slope to be skied. In some cases, you may even need to climb uphill. In deep snow this is time consuming, hard work, and more to the point, a situation for potential danger. The person cutting the track is doing the work, taking the risk, and entitled to first tracks.

When the track is being cut, it is imperative that the skiers behind remain patient and allow the track-cutter to do their work. Once you start to follow, the track will become faster with each skier and you must maintain a safe spacing. Once you regroup it is only polite to allow the track-cutter to open the slope. And if it was a group in front of you that did the work, there is no question about waiting patiently for them to open the slope and allowing them to move to a safe place before your group starts its descent.

It is incredibly frustrating when you take the risk and cut a track while your group is patiently waiting, to have another group use your track, almost elbowing your team members out of the way, and then dive down and take first tracks. This is the personification of impatience, bad manners and lack of respect. It does happen and the stress it causes within a group is enough to ruin your day.

I witnessed just such a case of rude behaviour during the big snow period of the 1998-99 season. We had just passed the Col Pers and were traversing off to the right in knee-deep snow. There were a couple of exposed places with loaded slopes above us, so extreme caution, patience, and good spacing were in order. Chris's group was behind mine; patiently waiting while I cut the track and my group could start traversing across. There were unfortunately a few impatient skiers behind us who were trying to cut up Chris's group and force their way past. Chris tried to give them a little lesson in etiquette but sadly his words fell on deaf ears. They eventually succeeded in bullying their way through by which time my group had moved on, but they had succeeded in stressing Chris's clients and putting a damper on their ambience.

The Col Pers is a vast area with an unlimited choice of fall-lines to choose from. Why these skiers had to push pass Chris I don't know, but they eventually skirted around us and made their own way down. We were all glad to see the back end of them and settled down to enjoying our descent.

Later that day there was an avalanche that claimed the life of one skier. As it happened, it turned out to be one of the impatient skiers who had muscled his way past Chris, all in a hurry to get on with his day.

Good last day behaviour

Just because it may be the last day of your holiday is no reason to drop your standards of good behaviour. Many skiers can be seen trashing snow with unrestrained enthusiasm because their holiday is coming to an end. They will not be there tomorrow so why not? It is only respectful to the environment and to other skiers who will still be there tomorrow and next week, to try to manage the snow properly, whether it is the first or last day of your holiday.

Silence is Golden

The mountains can be a very quiet and peaceful place. Unfortunately, some people seem to think that the more noise they make, the more fun other people will think they are having. These are usually the same people who insist on skiing powder slopes ten at a time, while fanning out to track out as much of the mountain as possible.

Photo 28, Plate section 2.

I ask my groups to stay quiet so that we can all concentrate on what is happening around us. If I am opening a slope I may say, "Please be quiet unless the mountain lets go". Then a yell from above could give me the warning I might need. I expect people only to make noise if there is some sort of problem, and then everyone in the group would immediately be alerted. A quieter atmosphere also gives you a chance to hear any signs that the snowpack may be giving you.

You sometimes see unaware people whistling or shouting at the wildlife, and this can be very harmful to their well-being. They have a long, tough winter and sometimes have just enough reserves to survive until spring.

The last thing a nervous chamois needs is to be frightened into a long run up the other side of the mountain to flee a screaming tourist. It can be enough to exhaust them and bring on an unnecessary death.

The mountains are a much more enjoyable place in silence. In the quiet calm you can feel the pulse and power of the environment and hear your own heartbeat. Please, keep the noise down.

Watch your step

Often when tracking across to access a slope you will come across ground that has been exposed. During the winter this may be a ridge that has had the snow swept away by the wind. But, as spring wears on, the snowpack visibly recedes from one day to the next as more and more ground becomes bared.

At first glance you may see nothing but dried up brown grass showing through. But, upon closer inspection, you may discover a micro-world teeming with plant life. Plant lovers would be astounded by the variety of plants that can be found within a square metre. The flora survives in the harshest of environments, but are still fragile to the trampling of heavy ski boots.

When setting a track for my clients I'll often stay in the snow and walk along the edge of the exposed ground to avoid our group needlessly walking over top of the plant life. At times there is no choice but to walk through a bared area. But, if you are aware and tread carefully, it is possible to avoid most of the plants and to keep the damage to a minimum.

Photos 29 and 30, Plate section 2.

Chapter Eight

Snow Management

Powder snow

POWDER SKIING is truly one of the great joys of skiing. To ensure maximum enjoyment for yourself, your group, and others skiing in the vicinity, it is important to make the most of the snow conditions. Powder snow is a precious commodity. It is not infinite; once it is tracked up it is gone. So it is frustrating to watch snow being needlessly (selfishly) wasted because it may be weeks before the next snowfall. We all want to ski fresh untracked snow. Not only today, but also tomorrow, the day after, and the day after that. And if all skiers were aware of snow management and made an effort, one snowfall could leave us with many, many more days of good skiing.

Start close to home

Because powder snow is like gold dust, I try to start with what is there, right in front of me, and then start to work further afield as the snow is tracked and used up. When guiding, there is no reason to cut the track or traverse across the slope any farther than necessary. If there is good snow at the edge of the face, ski it. Most people are frightened to open a big slope and will wait for someone else to take the risk. People will instantly follow tracks when they see a slope has been skied, but they are very reluctant to make the first track in and test the waters for themselves. The moment there is a set of tracks, everyone feels safe and the 'powder frenzy' is on. If you traverse further than you need to, the followers will track everything from the start of the face to where you have laid the first tracks.

A good example of this occurred several seasons ago in the Combe de Signal bowl at the Fornet. My group was the first up the Poma, and we had the chance to open the bowl. There were forty centimetres of wonderfully light powder, and my heart was beating away in my chest. I skied down immediately after ducking under the rope. We had face shots all the way to the bottom, rejoined the piste, and then circled back to do another run.

By the time we arrived back at the summit, about 20 minutes had passed. But, in the meantime, no one had taken the track further than we had. We traversed in a little further, next to our previous set of tracks, and started down again. Five or six runs later, we were still pushing the traverse a little further each time, but no further than needed to get fresh snow. Had I traversed halfway across the bowl on our first descent, half the face would have been tracked by the time we arrived for our second run.

Starting close to home also gives time to test the snow and develop a 'feel' for the conditions. This includes starting on or near the piste where you can warm up in total safety, while observing the stability of neighbouring slopes.

Keep your tracks close

Once you get to where you want to ski, keeping your team's tracks close together is the easiest and most effective way of making powder snow last. If your group lays its tracks side by side, you will be amazed at how little space you take up, while still allowing each skier fresh snow in which to leave their 'mark'. There is nothing more annoying than arriving at a beautiful slope that has been ruined by four skiers (or two surfs), one who has gone left, another who has veered right, and two that have zigzagged down the middle. The space taken by four could have accommodated 30 skiers making an effort to manage the snow.

At Alpine Experience we insist that our clients keep their tracks tight. This allows three or four groups to ski a slope instead of one. It permits us to come back for a second run or more, or save some untracked snow for another day. If necessary, we can get seven skiers down a space no wider than two-and-a-half metres across.

Photo 31, Plate section 3.

Keeping next to the track is also a great teaching aid. It helps people to find the timing that the slope and snow dictate. It develops flexion, extension, and linked movements. We are amazed at how quickly someone can learn to ski deep snow by concentrating on skiing next to a well-laid track. Keeping the track gives you something to strive towards and you can take great pride in being able to leave such an artistic signature on the mountain.

Ski the true fall-line

Another way to save snow is to ski the true fall-line. I have seen tracks where the skier, for some unknown reason, skied either left-to-right, or right-to-left diagonally across the true fall-line. I can't quite figure out why people do this but it happens frequently and is very annoying to find a slope cut in two by tracks across the fall-line. It means that to ski fresh snow and find the true fall-line you need to traverse one way or the other, leaving what could have been clean snow behind.

What if you can't link turns in the fall-line?

If you can't link turns in the fall-line, you really shouldn't be skiing powder off-piste. Because each time you shoot off across the mountain or fall over, there is an increased chance of triggering a slide. As far as snow management goes, you are wasting good snow and would be better off, and probably safer, to practice near the edge of the piste or in cut-up snow.

Spring snow

Spring is the highlight of the season for many skiers. It feels good to shed a layer of clothing and to be able to have lunch on a sun-drenched terrace. But what really makes spring so special is 'spring snow' itself.

The melt-freeze process, as a result of high temperatures during the day and negative temperatures at night, creates this phenomenal surface. The sun melts down the surface of the snowpack leaving it saturated with water that re-freezes into a solid mass at night. The result is a surface as flat as a billiard table. The snow is perfectly smooth and firm underneath, with the sun's rays creating a cushion of soft snow on the surface that is ideal for easy turning and edge control. Spring snow is by far the most flattering of all off-piste conditions, and there is not a piste machine in the world that can prepare a surface as perfectly as nature's own spring snow.

Unfortunately, like powder, spring snow also needs managing. It needs a chance to be created and then needs nurturing to make it last. A perfect spring slope can be ruined in one day by skiers who do not understand the necessary approach to spring snow. Here are some ways to maximise your enjoyment in the spring.

Give spring snow a chance

To enjoy spring snow it must first be created, and too often these days nature does not get the chance to transform fresh snow into that immaculate spring surface. Once spring arrives it is very important to ski powder snow only on northern exposures after a snowfall, and allow the sunnier exposures a chance to transform to spring snow. By skiing the sunny exposures (east, south, and western slopes) you will be leaving deep powder-type tracks that will refreeze at night and leave un-skiable ruts for the days that follow. These ruts will render the slope un-skiable until the next snowfall can cover the tracks, and give the mountain and nature another chance at creating spring snow.

How many days you may need to remain patient depends on the amount of fresh snow, the orientation of the slope, altitude and the strength of the sun. Six inches of fresh snow on a southern exposure, followed by strong sun may take only one day to transform back to spring snow. The same six inches of snow on an eastern slope will take a little longer to transform because the early morning sun is not as intense as the mid-day or afternoon sun. Altitude also plays a part. The higher you go, the cooler the temperatures are, and the longer it takes for snow to transform. So fresh snow at 2000 metres will transform to spring snow faster than new snow at 3000 metres. Finally, the more fresh snow that has fallen, the longer it takes to transform. But, with the intense sun of spring, the wait can be as little as one day and usually not more than three or four.

Besides giving Mother Nature a chance to work her wonders, you will also be safer and ski a much better quality of powder on northern slopes. Because the northern exposures are protected from the sun, the snow will stay cold, and therefore lighter, for much longer. The sun will affect the east, south, and western slopes and heat up the fresh snow. These slopes will hence offer much warmer snow that will be thicker and heavier, and much less enjoyable to ski. The added warmth will also add weight to the snowpack making these exposures more prone to avalanche.

If you remain patient for a day or two and stay on northern exposures after a snowfall, you will ski much better powder snow, in safer conditions, and give nature the time she needs to work her wonders.

Arrive on time

The key to conserving spring snow is to arrive on time. This is easier said than done, and is an art in itself. The trick is to arrive on a slope so that the sun has melted the top centimetre or two, giving you a soft cushion on top of the frozen support layer. If you arrive on time, the track left behind will be almost non-existent, and the afternoon sun will melt it down, leaving another perfect surface the following day. This meltdown is known as the healing process. But, if you arrive late on a slope, the snow will be too soft and the skis will push much more snow around. This results in leaving ridges and much deeper tracks that the afternoon sun cannot heal. These ridges and tracks will then refreeze at night leaving a rough, bone-jarring surface that is very unpleasant to ski.

Skiers who arrive even later cause more damage still. If you turn up and the support layer has already melted, instead of staying on the surface you will drop through up to the ankles or deeper. This makes skiing impossible and the only way out is kick turns and traverses all the way to the bottom. This scars the slope beyond repair and after the freeze at night, the next day brings frozen 'railway tracks' that are totally un-skiable. To arrive after the support layer has melted is also dangerous because that is when a spring slope is most prone to avalanche. This is especially true if there is a grassy slope underneath, because water will trickle down through the snowpack onto the grass below. That water will lubricate the grass, making it greasy, and a very good sliding surface.

Note: There is an added danger to spring snow if you arrive too early and the sun hasn't had a chance to soften the surface layer sufficiently. Instead of dream-like conditions you will confront hard icy snow that is difficult to edge. This is the worst possible snow to fall and slide on, and command of the self-arrest would be essential.

How to arrive on time

To ski perfect spring snow throughout the day you need to start on east facing slopes, which soften with the first sun of the day, then move onto south-east, south, south-west, and then western and northern slopes as you follow the sun's path across the sky.

But each day's timing can be different depending on climatic conditions, expositions and altitude. For example, with a minimum freeze at night followed by a strong sun the next morning, you might decide to miss out on the eastern slopes. Because the snow did not freeze as deeply, the support layer on the eastern slope will have melted early with the sun's first rays, and you may go directly to the southern exposures, skiing them at 9:30 where the day before you skied the same southern slope at 11:00. Or, if you had a good freeze followed by a sunny day with a cool breeze, the wind would slow down the softening process allowing you to ski an eastern slope at 10:15 when the same slope was too soft at 9:30 the day before.

Even a slight change of exposure on the same slope can make an enormous difference to the texture of the snow, and most slopes have varying aspects to play with. For example, if you were skiing on a southern slope, on a southeastern aspect and found that the snow was too soft, you could change exposures and find firmer snow. By moving from a southeastern to a southern aspect, the snow would be a little firmer, and if you moved to a southwestern aspect, the snow would be firmer still. If you were skiing a western slope, on a WNW aspect, and found that the snow was too hard, you could change aspects and find softer snow. If you moved back from WNW to west, the snow would be a little softer, and a move to WSW would find even softer snow still. Many slopes have ridges or gullies, which give important changes in exposures and drastic changes in snow. Other slopes offer only slight changes of aspect that are more delicate to play with, and yield subtler changes in snow.

Altitude also plays a major role in judging when to ski which slope. It is warmer at lower altitudes, so lower slopes will develop enough moisture to transform with negative temperatures to spring snow before the slopes at the cooler higher altitudes. In this case you may be able to ski spring snow on a southern slope at 1900 metres or less, early in the morning, and then go higher up and ski powder snow on northern exposures. That same southern exposure at 3000 metres may not have had enough moisture to transform to spring snow, but just enough to leave a breakable crust. With each successive spring day, the sun will transform the snow higher and higher up the mountain, and on different exposures, until eventually even the northern slopes will transform.

Another example would be after a mild night when the freeze level was at 2400 metres. There would be no point in trying to ski a slope that descends much below that level, especially on east or south facing slopes. You would need to go to higher altitude slopes, test the snow, and make a decision as to what exposure would be the best to start on. I constantly check the firmness and depth of freeze with my pole on different aspects to give me a clue to what exposure I need to ski next. Testing also helps me avoid arriving on a slope too early when the surface layer will still be frozen, and helps me judge how far down the mountain I can safely ski before the support layer becomes too fragile and eventually gives way.

How well it freezes at night and the following day's climatic conditions continually vary. How you play with the exposures and altitude can make the difference between skiing perfect spring snow, and icy or dangerously soft un-skiable snow. And having a daily presence in the mountains helps make these judgements so much easier.

Whether it is delicate spring snow or fragile wind-blown snow, the idea is to leave a clean, unbroken surface behind, so that the slope remains unmarked and perfect for the following day.

If you do arrive late...

Judging spring snow perfectly is an art. To judge it correctly day-in and day-out is difficult. Eventually you will get it wrong and the snow will be too soft. In this case, instead of skiing untracked snow and ruining that line for the following day(s), ski in old tracks and preserve the clean snow for another day. Because the snow is already too soft, you will get the same feeling underfoot skiing in the tracked snow as in the clean snow. You will not get the same visual effect, but this is when you should respect the mountain, and other skiers, and do the right thing.

If you arrive and the support layer is fragile and you are starting to break through, look for snow that has been skied on previous days. Snow that has been previously skied upon is packed and denser, and freezes more solidly than an un-skied spring surface. If you are breaking through on clean untracked snow, the tracked snow of yesterday may just keep you afloat.

Traversing

It is amazing how much damage can be caused by traverse marks. Generally, everyone in a group should take the same traverse. This is a safer way of moving about and is also much cleaner. I have seen slopes that have been traversed from one side to the other (sometimes 200metres across) and the entire slope has been ruined by traverse marks. This is a waste of powder and in the spring it makes for very unpleasant, bone-jarring skiing because of the refrozen tracks.

Chapter Nine

Tips and Techniques

NO MATTER what type of skiing you wish to do, you will only advance as far as your fundamental base will allow. It is impossible for you to reach your full potential if your basic skill level is lacking. Today there is a huge and varied range of skis designed to make skiing easier, but these new skis only mask one's technical deficiencies. Eventually, the lack of basics will show through. And nowhere in skiing is good technique as important as off-piste.

Where you can ski, and in what conditions, are directly linked to your skill level. The better your fundamental skills, the less restrictions you have in choice of terrain, allowing you to travel and ski in more interesting and exciting places. There are many different textures and densities of snow, and the better your technique, the more variations of snow you can handle comfortably and the easier it is for you to protect yourself from injury. Being able to adapt your technique can also allow you to help minimise the stress on the snowpack, which is critical for safe skiing when the conditions are suspect. Good technique simply gives you a wider choice of terrain and fewer limitations in the snow conditions that you can safely ski.

To give 'technique' the attention it deserves (to be properly described and fully understood) is worthy of a book in itself. So, what follows instead is only a 'shell' of the technique that I teach. It should, however, point you in the right direction. The simple, but to the point, tips in each section are basic pointers that can make an enormous difference to your safety and enjoyment.

I like to break skiing down into three main categories:
1. Timing (with flexion and extension),
2. Hip position (including upper and lower body independence), and
3. Balance (over the downhill ski's centre, or, pivot point).

With good timing, well placed hips and good balance over the outside (downhill) ski, you can initiate a turn where the skis will connect into the next turn automatically by an 'uncoiling' effect from the lower body. On the groomed piste the skis will turn by themselves, as if by magic. It is totally effortless and this 'uncoiling' is something I search for in each and every turn. Off-piste, where the snow textures and densities vary, 'uncoiling' greatly aids in the initiation of the turn, and steering takes the skis the rest of the way. 'Uncoiling' helps makes skiing smooth and graceful, while drastically reducing joint stress and fatigue.

Timing

The key to good timing is patience. Most skiers are in an incredible rush, coming up much too quickly and then coming down too early. Their movements are often abrupt and almost panicky.

I try to get skiers to slow their movements down by imagining themselves in a 'slow-motion' video. The projection (from the hips) and extension, or 'up' (for lack of a word that properly describes the movements) is smooth and continues until the fall-line. If you have come to your full height before the fall-line, you have come 'up' too quickly. From the fall-line you start a progressive 'down motion' that must last until the end of the turn. During this 'down motion' (again using 'down' for lack of a better one-word description) the steering must also continue until the end of the turn in order to make a round turn. 'Uncoiling' and steering takes you to the fall-line and continued steering during the 'down motion' finishes the turn.

Hip Position

Proper hip position is critical to smooth, effortless and efficient skiing. To develop good hip position it is imperative to have a tall stance, and be tension-free and independent between the upper and lower body.

The hips should always be facing downhill at the end of a turn, while the skis have been steered past the fall-line back uphill. The hips and upper

Photo 31: *Amount of space taken by three groups. My team has left the frame, TJ is leading his group out, and Chris's clients are still skiing the slope in the background. We have left clean untracked snow for whoever may be behind us, and plenty of room for ourselves if we fancy another run.* Photo Wayne Watson.

Photo 32: *Starting to finalise the ready position in the last third of the turn.*

Photo 33: *A strong 'ready' position in action off La Leisse near La Grande Motte.*

Photo 34: *A totally quiet upper body. The hands, and arms are in a comfortable position where they can aid balancing.*

Retraction Series on Steep Slope

Taken on the steep Pointe Pers in slightly compacted snow. The pitch and the snow conditions were ideal for exaggerated retraction.

Photo 24a:
Completing previous turn and finalising 'ready' position.

Photo 24b:
Upper body is facing between the pole and tips and the feet are being retracted back underneath the body.

Photo 24c:
'Uncoiling' and steering have started the turn, and the steering continues as the legs are reaching out to the side (or extending) en route to the fall-line.

Photo 24d:
Coming 'down' progressively and steering the skis back across the body, increasing the independence between upper and lower body.

Pole Plant Series

A sequence showing the timing of the pole plant along with the positioning of the hands and arms.

Photo 36a:
Just entering the last third of the turn and the pole is being prepared. The only movement is a bending at the elbow and wrist.

Photo 36b:
The pole is being planted while the left arm is totally still.

Photo 36c:
The body is projecting 'up' and through the 'door'. Both arms are in front and visible.

Photo 36d:
Just passing the fall-line and the left wrist is bending and the pole is moving forward in preparation. The right arm is quiet and stays in front.

Photo 36e:
Finalising the 'ready' position and the pole is just about to be planted.

Photo 37:
Widen your stance - the steeper the slope the wider the stance.

Stem Turn Series

Taken on fragile spring snow.

Note how both skis are weighted to help distribute the weight and avoid breaking through.

Photo 38a:
This is the 'ready' position in a stem. The uphill ski is already pointing in the direction of the turn and is also on the new inside edge. The moment of pivoting and changing the edges has been avoided.

Photo 38b:
The pole is in and the upper body is projecting 'up' and to the inside of the turn.

Photo 38c:
Approaching the fall-line and the wedged foot is starting to come parallel as the right foot is taking more weight.

Photo 38d:
Have come through the fall-line with the skis parallel again and ready to repeat the process.

Photo 39: *The late Giles Green demonstrating a strong classic jump turn in a steep couloir off la Pointe du Lavachet. A strong pole plant, retraction of the downhill ski, and a positive lift-off from the uphill foot.*

Photo 40: *...and when the going gets really steep. Jean Marc preparing to rope his clients down.*

Retraction Series on Fragile Spring Snow

Taken high up on the northern side of Combe du Signal. Again, distributing the weight is important on fragile snow.

Photo 41a:
Here the pole initiates the movements.

Photo 41b:
Bottom foot retracts; the jump comes from a gentle push off uphill foot combined with a retraction. 'Uncoiling' helps but the feet must be pivoted while airborne.

Photo 41c:
Landing in a high position with weight on both feet. Note the pole is still in the snow and has stabilised the upper body through the turn.

Photo 41d:
Slowly coming down and progressively increasing the grip on the mountain. Controlling momentum and building a platform from which to launch the next turn.

body are facing downhill and independent of the lower body, which is facing across the fall-line. And it is this independence and position of the hips, which create the 'uncoiling'. The upper body remains quiet and facing downhill while flowing (or projecting) into the next turn, and the feet and legs unwind back downhill as the next turn is initiated.

The more exaggerated the independence between the upper and lower body, the more 'uncoiling' or automatic pivoting will occur in the next turn. In a long radius turn, where the pivoting is slow and easy, the hips are barely facing downhill, thus producing minimal 'uncoiling'. In a short radius turn, where the pivoting and independence of upper and lower body are exaggerated, the hips are facing the fall-line giving maximum 'uncoiling'.

The upper and lower body are never 'fused' together, but the separation between the two can be very subtle. Hip placement begins to change the instant a new turn is initiated. The moment the turn begins, the hips, which were facing downhill, start to open to the downhill side of the new turn. This opening of the hips is incredibly discreet in a long turn but becomes more noticeable as the turns shorten. The final placement of the hips develops progressively from the fall-line towards the end of the turn. From the fall-line, the feet continue to turn back uphill independently of the hips and upper body. During the 'down' motion, the steering of the feet back uphill is maximised, exaggerating the independence between the upper and lower body.

How far uphill the skis are turned and how much the hips are left facing downhill depends on the radius of the next turn. In long radius turns the hips continue to follow the skis around from the fall-line towards the end of the turn, and the increase in separation between upper and lower body comes late in the turn and the separation is minimal. Minimal separation creating minimal 'uncoiling'. In short radius turns the hips do not follow the skis around at all. The hips remain facing the fall-line while the skis are steered back and forth across the body. This will create the most exaggerated form of independence between the upper and lower body, and produce the maximum 'uncoiling' effect, which will quickly bring the skis back through the fall-line in the next turn.

Balance

The final part of this basic equation is being properly balanced over the downhill ski's pivot point. The closer you stand over the ski's centre, or 'magic' pivot point, the easier life becomes. The easier it will be to control your momentum from the previous turn and the more effortless and cleaner the link into the next turn will be. The further away you stand from the ski's centre the less control you will feel and, because you will be working against the ski's construction design, the more difficult and forced the initiation of the next turn will be.

A good stance

Developing a good stance is critical for giving yourself the best chance to make real progress and maximise your potential. A good stance allows the body to function efficiently. Without a good stance it is difficult to relax, and any tension will inhibit the body from moving freely and fluidly. I am a firm believer in standing 'tall'; being centred over the downhill ski's pivot point, and being tension-free from the head down to the toes and finger tips. I also stress concentrating on the feet and ankles. The ankle is the first joint up from the ski and does much more work than most skiers realise. The ankles start the flexion and extension, and the feet and ankles help create edge and steering.

The advantages of a tall stance are numerous. When standing tall you benefit from a full range of leg movement for absorbing bumps and uneven terrain, and for retracting and extending in deep powder. From a tall position you are in total control, able to remain patient with all your 'down' motion left for when you are ready to finish the turn. By staying tall you give yourself a chance to be 'independent' in the upper and lower body, allowing you to angulate and benefit from 'uncoiling'. Skiing tall also conserves energy because the muscles are not contracted, allowing you to ski longer while helping to eliminate that next-day muscle stiffness. A tall stance allows you to ski from your feet and ankles instead of the knees, which protects your knees from injury. Skiers who crouch over (or are broken at the waist) will block themselves from properly placing the hips, and will therefore lose the 'uncoiling' effect. Breaking at the waist also overloads the tips making it difficult to control the tail of the skis. Crouching over also exposes the lower back to unnecessary stress, which often leads to back pain.

The key to developing a tension-free stance is to concentrate on settling the body's mass down into the feet. When standing correctly you should be as comfortable and unrestricted as standing in a pair of tennis shoes. Most skiers have tension somewhere in their body, whether it is in the legs, hips, back, shoulders, arms, wrists, or perhaps the neck.   By standing tall and letting the body's weight, plus the pressure of centrifugal force that builds through the turn, bypass the knees and settle down into the feet, you can eliminate any unnecessary stress on joints.

From a 'tall', centred, tension-free stance you will be readily able to adapt to changes of terrain and snow conditions. You will be able to ski as powerfully as you desire, benefit from the ski's construction, and ski efficiently while drastically reducing fatigue and stress on the knees and lower back.

The 'ready' position

See Photos 32 and 33 in Plate section 3.

Whether skiing on or off-piste, what I call the 'ready position' is the ideal base, or platform, from which to initiate a turn with the aid of automatic pivoting, or 'uncoiling'. The position is created during your 'down motion', and finalised in the last third of the turn.   The hips will be left facing downhill between the pole and ski tips, and the body weight centred over the downhill ski's pivot point, and out over the mountain (over the downhill ski as compared to banking uphill).

In a turn, the 'down motion' is the last chance to stabilise yourself and find the magic pivot point.   During this phase you are progressively increasing your grip on the mountain while continuing to steer the skis through to the end of the turn. You are controlling the momentum from the last turn while stabilising yourself and creating a moving platform from which to initiate the next turn. The more stable the platform, the more in control you will feel. And the closer you are to the pivot point with your balance, the easier the next turn will be. This moving platform, with the hips facing downhill between the pole and ski tips, the weight centred and through the feet, and the pole prepared and ready to plant, is the 'ready position'. And if you find the skis' pivot point, the next turn will just happen, smoothly and effortlessly.

A to Z

I first arrived in Europe as a dynamic, edge-to-edge skier, and tried to ski powerfully and carve my way through every type of snow that I encountered. Then one day something happened, and a few words from someone else started me thinking, and I've never looked at skiing the same way since.

We were skiing the steep North Face of the Bellecôte in 40 centimetres of fresh snow, and my friend Biggy was really struggling. TJ then said to him, "Biggy, have you ever tried side-slipping in powder?" Biggy, a proud edge-to-edge man himself, snorted out, "NO!" TJ paused for a few moments; letting his words sink in before calmly replying, "You ought to try it sometime." Since then, I've looked at skiing as having an 'A' to 'Z' of edge control, and think of 'A' as a flat ski with minimum edge and 'Z' as a maximum edged ski.

Imagine a flat minimally-edged ski in the snow. It is easily pivoted, making it easy to manoeuvre and steer.

Now imagine an edged ski in the snow. This one will not pivot and will follow an arc that is largely dictated by the skis side-cut. (An over-edged ski will neither pivot nor follow an arc, and tends to run straight. This is the moment when the knees are at risk in tricky snow.)

In skiing there is a time and a place for every 'touch' between 'A' and 'Z', and having the full range of edge control at your command is invaluable in adapting to changes in snow and terrain.

Unfortunately, over the past 15 years, and more so since the invention of the 'carvers', most skiers seem obsessed with edging their skis as much as possible. Skier's end up one dimensional, having a limited range of edge control. A Z-type approach works in certain conditions, but snow off-piste often calls for a softer touch, and it can be imperative to be able to make the adjustment towards a flatter A-type ski when conditions dictate. One of the most common mistakes we see guiding off-piste comes from good experienced piste skiers who lack a full range of edge control. They try to force their limited 'Z' technique on snow that requires anything but an over-edged ski. They find it frustrating to learn that the hard-edge approach they have had drummed into their thought process is undermining their progress in deep and varied snow. Trying to impose your will on the mountain rarely works.

TJ's words to Biggy have resulted in me changing my definition of what a carved turn is. In skiing, any round turn is a good turn. The often unappreciated round, gliding, flat A-type turn, is really the 'grandfather' of the carved turn. When you look at the track of a perfectly carved turn, you will see a clean arc in the snow. If you look at the track of a gliding flat ski turn the track will be much wider than that of the arced 'line' left by the carving ski. But, if the tail of the skis have been controlled, there will be a clean arc left at the bottom of the track. It will not be as deep as the track left by the 'Z' ski, but the arc will be just as clean. I now feel, and many skiers do not appreciate this, that any round turn *is* a form of a carved turn. Furthermore, it takes more skill to steer a flat ski into a round turn while controlling the tails, than it does to just simply roll the ski onto an edge and let the side-cut do the work.

One of the biggest contrasts between a flat 'A' ski and an edged 'Z' ski can be found in deep snow. A flatter ski will float, and can be steered. An edged ski can easily dig in and dive, and often runs straight. A flat ski is much more efficient in controlling your speed. An edged approach tends to be much quicker and, more often than not, off-piste conditions call for slower, controlled skiing. Another contrast is on fragile spring snow. A flatter ski can caress the eggshell type surface while an over-edged ski will break through. Skiers lacking the skill of steering a flat ski through a round turn will fall in just about each turn on fragile snow. Fragile snow is one of the best 'teachers' in skiing, and people must make changes to their approach or they are going to be totally miserable.

Retraction

See Photo series 35 in Plate section 3.

There is another extreme range of contrary skills necessary for safe off-piste skiing. On the piste and especially when skiing aggressively, you will be putting pressure into the snow. The more aggressive and dynamically you ski, the more extreme the pressure you will apply. But off-piste there are often situations when it is imperative to be able to retract, or pull the feet up underneath you, and take pressure out of the snow. One such time is when the snowpack is suspect and you are wondering about the stability of the mountain. You will need to stay as light as possible through the turn, especially towards the end of the turn where the pressure naturally builds. The last thing you need is to stress the snowpack by pounding down to finish each turn. Each thump into the snow is a potential trigger for starting a slide. Instead of pressuring the snow at the end of the turn you should retract the feet, relieving pressure from the snow, and keeping the stress on the snowpack to a minimum.

Another such example is in fragile, spring snow. It really can be as delicate as skiing on eggshells. Besides needing to be able to pivot and steer throughout the turn to distribute the weight, it is essential to be able to retract the feet and minimise the pressure in the snow. Fragile snow can undoubtedly be the inadaptable 'Z' skier's worst nightmare.

Don't get me wrong. Dynamic skiing is fun. You feel strong and use the power in the ski to a maximum. Harnessing and directing this energy is very exciting. There is definitely a time and place for aggressive skiing. In fact, it is a very important part of skiing. But, when conditions call for a softer touch, a versatile skier with a full range of edge control will be able to make the necessary adjustments.

Developing a full 'A' to 'Z' of edge control is crucial for protecting your knees from injury and adapting to the various snow conditions that will be encountered off-piste.

The Basic Flow

Study the diagram on page 136, over, and refer to it often.

In skiing, one turn links into the next. Imagine A as the path that the skis travel, B represents the path that the body follows to the inside of the turn and C represents the last third of the turn.

This phase C is your last chance to stabilise yourself over the pivot point as you complete the turn, and create a good 'ready' position. The closer you can get to perfecting your balance during phase C, the smoother the events at point D will be.

Point D is where all the action takes place and one turn connects into the next. It is where you arrive at your lowest. In the 'ready' position, your hips are facing between the prepared pole and your downhill ski tip. Imagine this space as a door. At point D the hips flow or project, through the door into the next turn, and the feet come under the body and out the other side, *en route* to the fall-line. This is the beginning of the extension. And the extension (or up) is really just skiing the skis from your lowest position (D) to the fall-line (E), where you are at your tallest position during the turn.

One of the keys to flowing skiing is controlling the tail of the skis. No matter what you are doing on your skis, whether it is side-slipping, or any type of turn between 'A' and 'Z', the goal is to control the tail of the downhill ski. The moment the tail slides away you have lost your 'grip' and your platform will be slipping away from you. If the tail gets away, the downhill leg becomes a brace, blocking the hips and upper body from flowing into

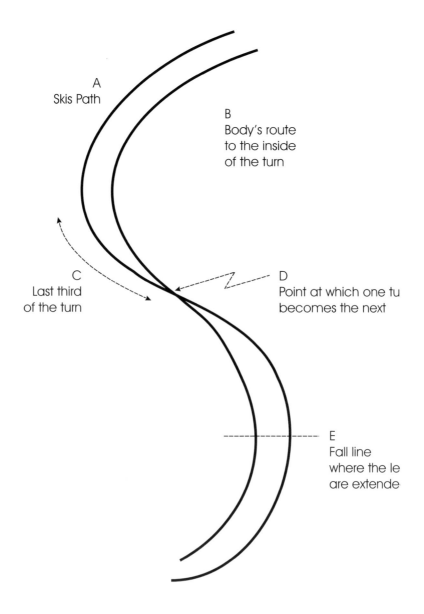

A
Skis Path

B
Body's route
to the inside
of the turn

C
Last third
of the turn

D
Point at which one tu
becomes the next

E
Fall line
where the le
are extende

the next turn. And once the flow into the next turn is blocked, mistakes are inevitable. Because the hips cannot move into the next turn, your only way out is a straight 'up' motion, a rotation, a stem, or a combination of any or all of these. Once the tails are sliding away your platform will be weak and unstable. You will not be in total control of your momentum, and getting off an unsteady platform and into the next turn will be forced instead of a smooth connection.

Hand and arm positioning

The positioning and movements of the 'hands' and 'arms' are incredibly important. They aid in your balance, in developing good timing, and in keeping the upper body well positioned and quiet. The upper body should be totally still and completely relaxed. All the 'action', such as 'up' and 'down', pivoting and steering, retracting, and absorbing uneven terrain, comes from the feet, ankles, and knees. It is like a Rolls Royce where the ride is totally smooth because the wheels and suspension are absorbing the bumps in the road. How you carry your hands and arms, and when and where you plant your poles, will go a long way in determining how quiet, stable, and comfortable the upper body will be, and help with the precision of your timing.

You must start by holding your hands and arms in a comfortable position. Neither too far apart nor too close together, and not too high and not too low. They must be held tension-free and in an athletic position, where they can aid your balance. *See Photo 34, Plate section 3.*

In any turn, no matter what the radius, the uphill hand must be visible from the bottom corner of your vision. If the uphill hand disappears back out of sight, it allows the upper body to rotate uphill. The elbows should be bent and held slightly 'in' towards the ribs as compared to slightly 'bowed'. The hands should be bent slightly 'out' at the wrists, which helps keep the elbows 'in' and 'locks' the hips in the proper position. When the hips are properly placed it is easier to 'grip' and create a good platform from which to 'uncoil'. If the hands are curled to the inside it allows the elbows to bow or 'fly out' (like wrapping your arms around a barrel). Usually when the elbows 'fly out' the hips follow, pulling them from a position of facing downhill into a rotation back uphill. This rotation is enough for the skis to lose their 'grip' causing you to lose the good platform needed to initiate the next turn. By rotating uphill you also lose the 'uncoiling' position and therefore your automatic pivoting. At all times the hands and arms should be tension-free.

The pole plant

See Photo series 36 in Plate section 3.

Where you plant your pole depends on the radius of the turn and is directly related to your hip position. In a long radius turn the pole is planted further towards the tips as the hips are barely facing downhill. As the turns become shorter and shorter, and the hips are facing more and more downhill, the pole plant comes further and further back.

The 'key' is to never reach towards the tips to plant your pole. In the 'ready' or 'uncoiling' position, the hips and upper body are facing between the pole and the ski tips. As I said before, imagine that space between the two as a 'door'. When initiating a turn the upper body flows, or projects, laterally through that 'door' into the new turn. When you reach with the pole you close the 'door' and block your projection, or flow into the new turn. Reaching has other adverse effects. Reaching can pull you forward onto your toes, which also allows the tails to 'wash-out', or slide away, resulting in a loss of grip and a stable platform.

How firmly the pole is planted is also related to the radius of the turn. The pole hardly touches the snow in a very long turn, if at all. At speed, you may make only a gesture with the downhill hand. As the turns become shorter, the pole plant becomes firmer. As the slope becomes steeper, the pole plant becomes more and more important in stabilizing the upper body. The pole is not however, there to be leaned upon. The only time you might 'hang', or lean on the pole, is when you make a mistake. The pole can give you a moment's grace, time enough to correct the problem and get the feet back underneath you. This is where skiers with a late pole plant have problems. By the time they prepare the pole to plant it and stabilize themselves, they have already fallen.

You have only one chance to link one turn to the next. Refer back to the diagram on page 136. Point D is where it all happens. If your pole plant is late you will miss the moment. On piste, skiers can usually get away with a late pole plant. But in deep or varied snow a well-timed pole plant is essential in properly connecting one turn to the next.

The key to developing good timing with the poles is to concentrate on the preparation. The start of the 'down' motion triggers the preparation of the pole. The elbow and wrist are bending up throughout the 'down' motion and as you come to your lowest position the pole is prepared and ready to plant. One of the most common mistakes we see in deep snow is a late and jerky pole plant. Skiers arrive at the bottom of the 'down' motion and the arms are down at their side, with the downhill (to be planted pole) pole still pointing behind them. By the time they fish out the pole, the moment and chance of linking the turn is long gone. Instead of smoothly connecting into the next turn, it is the first turn all over again.

Any unnecessary movement of your arms may disrupt your balance and have an effect on your contact with the snow. When planting the poles your arms should hardly move. There is a slight bending at the elbow of the downhill arm and the rest of the movement comes from the wrist. Meanwhile the uphill arm is relaxed and totally still. The timing with the pole preparation and pole plant is essential in avoiding abrupt and unnecessary movements which can cause a loss of 'grip' and your 'platform', and a loss of 'uncoiling.'

Spend some time on the piste concentrating on your hand and arm position, and your timing with the pole plant. The key for placement is to feel relaxed and comfortable, but at the same time athletic. As for timing, think of a slow controlled preparation that starts with the 'down' motion. It will be time well spent.

Chapter Ten

More Tips for Special Situations

Side-slipping

MY CLIENTS often hear the words, "If you can side-slip you can get down anything". Side-slipping is an invaluable skill off-piste. Not a day goes by where it is not used at some point, whether to enter or leave a slope, slow yourself down on a traverse, sneak through a narrow passage, avoid obstacles, or avoid turning on difficult snow or hazardous terrain. When someone has good side-slipping skills, their horizons broaden as to where they can travel and ski.

- When you feel the need to side-slip there is usually a good reason, such as something tricky to deal with. The first step is to widen your stance. (The steeper the terrain the wider the stance – *see Photo 37, Plate section 13*.)
- The upper body should be facing the direction of travel.
- The downhill pole should be pointing forward and prepared to plant. If you trip up a quick jab with the pole may be enough to stabilise yourself.
- When the snow is fragile try pointing your uphill ski slightly uphill. This increases the surface area in touch with the snow and helps to support your weight. The weaker the surface, the wider the stance. When dealing with fragile snow try to weight both skis.
- Diverging the uphill ski further uphill is also very effective on hard snow and ice.
- Both legs are capable of independent action. One leg may go up as the other leg goes down. Independent leg action gives you stability, much like independent suspension in a car.

- When side-slipping in deep or thick snow, lean uphill slightly and help yourself along by pushing off the uphill pole.

There is a time and place to side-slip. Know your limitations and when in doubt a side-slip is your safest way to deal with the problem.

Stem turns

See Photo series 38, Plate section 3.

Stem turns are another important option off-piste. No matter how experienced a skier you may be, there will come a time when the stem turn is your best, and sometimes only weapon. The beauty of this turn is that it avoids the delicate moment of pivoting and changing from one set of edges to the other.

- As you are lowering yourself and creating a platform on the downhill ski, start to slide your uphill ski away from you in a wedge shape.
- The 'ready position' will be the same except for the positioning of the uphill ski. The bottom foot is weighted, the hips are facing downhill, and the pole is prepared and ready to plant.
- Initiate the pole plant and project the hips forward and up, towards the inside of the new turn. The projection will take you onto the new ski, with the new ski heading in the direction of the new turn on the new edge. (The upper body stays to the inside of the new turn. You do not shift your weight back uphill to get onto the new ski). The moment of pivoting and of changing the edges has been avoided. The previously weighted foot can stay in the snow, but as the terrain becomes steeper it will be retracted (as in a jump turn).
- From a tall position in the fall-line, continue to steer during the down motion through to the end of the turn while creating a new platform from which to stem the uphill foot away, and then initiate the next turn.

Stem turns off-piste are an advanced manoeuvre. Do not be afraid to use them on steep slopes in place of a jump turn. They are also an excellent way of testing delicate snow to see whether or not you want to try pivoting from a parallel stance.

Jump turns

The moment of truth really is the moment of pivoting. It is at that moment where you risk catching an edge and falling headfirst. If you are not confident of your pivoting skills or the snow conditions, a jump turn can help enormously. There are several types of jump turns and how and where you use them depends on the conditions.

Jump turns can be a very effective way to initiate a turn. But they are not as easy as they may look, or sound. You must be able to control the tail of the downhill ski. If the bottom foot slides away, your platform will be weak and it will be next to impossible to initiate a safe jump turn.

Steep slopes compound the problem of creating a stable 'ready position'. If you cannot create a comfortable platform, use a stem turn instead. The goal is to get down in one piece and a stem turn is still one of the most useful tools in skiing. Steep slopes are no place to make mistakes, so when unsure, stem instead.

Like the self-arrest, practice jump turns on steep but short pitches, with a safe obstacle free reception zone.

Classic jump turns

These are the jump turns you will see in a 'ski extreme' video. They are used on steep slopes, and usually require a good surface from which to push off.

Photo 39, Plate section 3.

- You must first create a stable platform from which to initiate the turn. The tail of the downhill ski needs to be controlled. The pole must be prepared and ready to plant. And a positive attitude will help enormously. Basically you need to create the ultimate in a 'ready position'. Remember; never launch a turn in the steep until you feel totally comfortable.

- A strong pole plant initiates the movements. The pole is heavily relied upon during the initiation of turns on steep slopes. The hips (and upper body) start to move downhill into the new turn. As the body projects, the bottom foot retracts out of the snow, and the entire jumping action comes off the **uphill** foot. The firmer the snow, the easier it is to get a positive lift off. You push off the uphill foot but also pull, or retract the feet back up underneath you.

- 'Uncoiling' will help, but you must also turn the feet while airborne.

- The key now is to land in a high position (with your legs extended) and on a flat ski in a controlled side-slip. From a tall position you can slowly come down to soften the landing, while progressively increasing the edge and creating a platform for the following turn.* If you land on a hard edge in a low position, you are like a compressed spring. It won't take much for you to be rebounded headfirst downhill.

- Keep your feet apart. A wide stance and independence of legs is crucial in steep terrain.

* The more skilled and experienced the skier, the shorter the time frame needed to land, control the momentum, and create the next platform. An experienced skier may make fifteen controlled turns on a pitch where a less experienced skier may only have time to control two or three turns. Obviously, there would be much more side-slipping between turns from the inexperienced skier.

Retraction jump turns

See Photo series 41, Plate section 3.

Retraction jump turns are very similar to the classic turn, except they are used when there is not a firm surface to push off, or jump from. The retraction jump turn is invaluable on such surfaces as fragile spring or windblown snow.

- Use a wide stance. The wider the stance the bigger the surface area underneath you to support the body weight.
- The building of your platform must be very progressive and smooth. Any abrupt movement and you will break the surface and potentially trip up.
- The pole still triggers the turn, but it cannot be as relied upon as when skiing firm snow. Fragile snow will support a flat sliding ski but the pole will break through the surface layer if planted too firmly.
- Retract and pivot the feet. Suck the feet back up underneath you without stamping down on the bottom foot or pushing off the uphill ski. Again, any abrupt or firm pressure and you will break through.
- Land on both feet in a high (tall) position. Because the snow is fragile landing with weight on both feet helps distribute the body weight. If you land totally on the downhill ski you will break through immediately. Also land pivoting and sliding. Keep the skis turning and sliding through the fall-line. When sliding you are caressing the surface and minimizing weight and time spent on a particular bit of snow. If you land on an edge(s), or over-edge at any moment, you will break the fragile support layer and fall over.
- You are now back to slowly and progressively creating a platform from which to initiate the next turn.

Hop turns

See Photo series 42, Plate section 3.

Hop turns are used on gentler terrain when you are unsure of your ability to pivot the skis due to snow conditions. You will be making longer radius turns, and travelling quicker than on steeper slopes. Pivoting in longer turns is slow and easy, so the need for a jump with exaggerated pivoting is not necessary. All you need to do is get the pivoting started.

- Create a stable 'ready position'.
- Initiate a small hop, either by the classic or retraction approach. Remember, you are not trying to hop the skis all the way around. Just a change of direction and edges is all that is needed.
- Land tall and pivoting.
- Continue to steer the skis through to the end of the turn while creating your next platform from which to start the next turn.

Traversing

Traversing is a very necessary part of off-piste skiing. Frequently, you will need to move across a slope to gain access to the pitch that you want to ski. And often you will need to traverse after skiing a slope, to make your way back to civilisation.

Sometimes the slope that needs to be crossed is gentle. But, at other times, traversing can be very interesting to say the least. In fact, traversing is what many experienced off-piste skiers fear most.

Quite often, there will be intimidating terrain down below the traverse line. This usually gets skiers wondering what would happen if they fell off the traverse. And speed control can also be unsettling. The traverse line may be icy. It may be necessary to slow down or stop for unexpected bumps or dips, or for rocks that may become exposed because of the passage of previous skiers. All in all, there are often features, which may cause concern.

Traversing in powder snow

Sometimes it is necessary to climb while setting a traverse to access the area to be skied. This does not cause any technical problems. All you have to do is side step up the slope. But if you are not climbing it is a different story. It is important to choose the right angle of downward bias to cut the traverse line. You will find it hard work to cut a traverse in deep snow and it can be very tempting make it easy on yourself and use the slope to help you through the snow. Or, if unsure of the stability of the snowpack, you may want to cut a steeper traverse in order to spend less time exposed while making the track. For whatever reason, if the traverse is cut too steeply, it can have disastrous effects because it will become quicker with each skier who comes across. The last person across may be faced with a roller-coaster ride that they can't quite control, or get off. It is imperative to correctly judge the traverse line to safely keep the followers speed under control. And if you are worried about the stability of the slope, you probably should not be there.

- Cut a shallow path. The path will probably be shallower than you think. This comes with experience and if there is an existing traverse line that is suitable, use it. If it is too steep cut another track.
- Control your speed. The best tactic is to slow yourself down before you feel speed is a problem. 'Check' your speed at every opportunity. Once you are going too quickly in deep snow it is very difficult to slow down. Side-slip if the track is wide enough, or against the downhill edge of the path. Steer uphill into the deeper snow until you feel comfortable before dropping back onto the traverse. Again, this must be done before speed has become a factor, or you risk being spun around and thrown off the traverse. With experience you can learn to drag your uphill ski against the snow above the traverse line to help slow yourself.

● Let the person behind you know if there are any surprises waiting, such as bumps, dips, stumps or rocks (only if this can be done without risking your own balance or control).

Traversing on spring snow

It is still important to choose a line that will keep the speed comfortable for the weakest skier in the group. But, because you will stay on the surface of spring snow, the angle of the traverse line is not so important. You can easily adjust your speed by angling further uphill. You may however, come across other problems, such as the snow being too soft and not supporting, or icy.

● Control your speed. Angle more uphill, or side-slip.
● Avoid the sidewall of the traverse. Keep your ski tips away from the wall that builds up on a well-used traverse. The wall may be hard and icy, and it is very difficult to side-slip comfortably with your tips bouncing around off the wall. Instead, side-slip with your feet on the downhill side of the path. This may mean that the tail of your skis will be hanging over the edge, but it will be a smoother ride and you will be safer and stable.
● Concentrate and observe. Because the snowpack is melting down day by day, a traverse line will change daily. Rocks may appear that were not present the day before. These rocks can be jagged and enough to throw you off the traverse if you ski over them. And there could be intimidating circumstances below.

Should there be an existing path it can be used beneficially in a couple of ways.
● If the snow on the path is icy, stay above or drop below the existing path. The clean untracked snow will be softer and easier to grip on.
● If the snow is fragile use the existing path. The snow will be compacted and denser because it has been skied upon. The path will freeze harder and deeper at night and it will support longer into the next day, while the clean untracked snow beside it may be breaking through.

Staying away from the wall is a general traversing tip no matter what the snow conditions. You often see inexperienced skiers seeking safety close to the wall and getting their tips caught. It is like beginners feeling safer by leaning uphill, trying to get closer to the mountain. Both make sense to the inexperienced, but both tactics have negative results.

If you have a fear of heights, do not look down. Concentrate on the traverse path in front of you. If being properly guided you will be somewhere that you can technically handle.

Searching for a lost ski

Losing a ski is no fun. Looking for it can be tiring and time-consuming. It can also mean an entire group exposing themselves on a slope while searching for it. If you do not eventually find it, you can be left to struggle on one foot towards civilisation that may be a long way away. Losing a ski can also be costly. Not only do you need to buy a new pair of skis, but a new pair of bindings as well.

If you are an intermediate and not very confident about staying on your feet, try powder straps. These are long colourful ribbons that attach to the bindings and then tuck up under your ski-pant legs. When you fall and the ski(s) releases, the ribbon stretches out and trails the ski, and often remains on the surface.

Everyone falls at some stage and losing a ski is always a possibility when skiing deep snow. Here are some pointers for looking for that elusive ski(s).

- You should be concentrating (it might help keep you on your feet in the first place). When you fall try to be sensitive to what is happening under the snow. Did you come out of the heelpieces? Did you fall face first? If not, which way were you pointing when the ski released? The answer to these questions gives you a clue as to where to start.

- Survey the surface for clues. Is there a track running off to the side? Has the ski run below you?
- Check the track above you and determine where the ski(s) was last with you. How fast where you skiing? How steep is the slope? The faster you where skiing and the steeper the slope, the greater the search area will be.
- The first rule of thumb is that the ski(s) is usually much farther above you than first thought. Take off the other ski (if it is still with you) and climb back uphill towards the area you feel the ski may be. Use the tail of the ski to cut a grid in the snow. From where you are standing, cut the snow horizontally across the fall-line just above the boots. If the snow is light you can go right down to the heelpiece. Then lean forward and cut horizontally again about a foot higher. Keep working up in this fashion until you can no longer effectively reach any higher. Then cut vertically from one side to the other. This allows you to effectively cover a fairly large area. Keep moving up and systematically search each area until you find the ski. Stabbing around with your poles is useless.
- If you lose both skis, turn a pole upside down and cut the grid with your pole.

If you have companions to help, make sure they enter the search area carefully. If they trample the snow around you it packs the snow and makes cutting the grid much more difficult. Have them take a good look around for surface clues. Tell them how you fell and where you fell. Spread them out and search in an organised fashion, as above.

Getting it back on

There is always a moment's celebration when a probing searcher locates the missing ski. Companions are happy because they are keen to get on with the skiing again. The owner of the ski quickly adds up how much money he or she just saved, and the guaranteed smile brightens up their face. And the guide is thankful because they have been spared from the manly ritual of donating one of their skis to the cause and continuing down on one foot. But once you've found the ski you need to be able to get it back on. This can be easier said than done when standing on a steep slope in knee-deep snow.

The problem in deep snow is that every time you step down into the heelpiece the ski just sinks deeper into the snow. At the same time snow clogs up the heal mechanism, and it can become a vicious circle. The madder you become the harder you stamp down, sending the ski deeper into the snow and resulting in even more snow clogging up the heel piece. Fortunately, Giles Green came up with another neat trick to stop this situation from getting out of hand. It is really quite brilliantly simple.

- First, gently place the toe into the toe piece.
- Slowly lift the ski out of the snow. The tail will be slightly dropped and the ski will be balanced from the toe. *Photo 43a, Plate section 4.*
- Now gently lift the toes towards the sky while smoothly pressing down on the heel. The ski will snap back on, no fussing or cussing. *Photo 43b, Plate section 4.*

Try it on the piste. Once you get a feel for it you'll never need to struggle putting a ski on in deep snow again.

Chapter Eleven

Powder Skiing

DURING THE season the different types of snow that we encounter are uncountable and often inexplicable. The various textures and densities in snow between perfect powder and perfect spring are incredible. Easy snow is easy snow. You can get away with mistakes and your technique is not really tested. But as the snow becomes trickier (or more educational), your technique becomes more exposed.

There are several key points that always come to the forefront when teaching skiers off-piste. Patience and timing are essential. So is a good pole plant. The ability to keep the feet still and quiet in the snow and the ability to pivot and steer the skis through a round turn are critical. And if you can side-slip you will be able to get down anything safely, no matter how steep or narrow. You will hear these terms often and if they sound repetitious, it is because they are the basics of sound off-piste technique.

I will now give you some helpful advice for some of the various snow conditions and different terrain that you may find yourself in when off-piste. The types of snow mentioned will be very general, as there are hundreds of textures and densities within each category.

Powder snow

'Powder' is a loose term to describe deep, or soft snow, which is the most sought-after snow of all. It comes in many depths and consistencies, from a few centimetres on a firm base to waist deep (or deeper). It comes from ultra-light, dream snow to denser, wind-compacted or temperature-affected snow. Wind, temperature (both hot and cold), cloud cover, rain, humidity and sunlight can have an affect. But certain aspects of powder technique remain the same, no matter what the consistency.

Perhaps the most common advice given for powder skiing is to 'keep equal weight on both skis'. I do not entirely agree with this theory. In fact, I'm a firm believer that you often ski from one foot to the other in soft snow. Imagine a firm base with just three centimetres of fresh snow. You would ski left foot, right foot, left, right and so on just as you would on the piste. With six centimetres, you would still ski left, right, left, right but a little subtler from foot to foot. With ten centimetres a little subtler still. As the snow becomes deeper, the foot-to-foot pressure becomes more discreet until you come to a depth where you are more or less on one platform, or equally-weighted on both skis.

Unfortunately, one of the most common mistakes in deep snow is over pressuring the downhill foot. This will push the over-pressured ski down into the snow, while the un-weighted ski will float closer to the surface. This action will throw the skier off balance and leave them in an unstable and uncomfortable position. It will also kill the turn, stopping the pivoting and making it impossible to link turns. But, I feel that if you can keep your feet still in the snow, you will never be far from equally weighted skis. With quiet feet you can delicately apply the required foot-to-foot pressure dictated by the snow conditions. And when one platform is required, the adjustment is minimal.

'Quiet or still' feet are my version of equally weighted skis, but precisely applied foot to foot pressure is often used. Progressively applying the proper 'dose' of pressure from foot to foot without over pressuring one ski is a fine, precise skill. Stand tall, and being relaxed and calm will make acquiring this subtle skill much easier.

Photos 44a and 44b, Plate section 4.

Another of the keys to good powder skiing is that of linking round turns. The moment of truth in any turn is the moment of pivoting. The turn must be initiated positively. If you have created a moving 'ready position' over the pivot point and project properly into the new turn, the 'uncoiling' affect will greatly aid in a smooth initiation. And a properly timed pole plant will help in stabilising the upper body and triggering the new turn. As you are steering and skiing the skis towards the fall-line you will be arriving at

Dead Spots

A 'dead spot' in a turn occurs when there is a lack of connection in the body movements. It breaks your rhythm, allows the energy in the skis to dissipate, and inhibits you from linking turns. 'Dead spots' also tend to compound the problems of tricky snow. Once the skis are 'railing' it can be very difficult to get them pivoting again.

your full height. Now patience becomes a major factor - don't be in a hurry. The 'down' motion must be progressive. During this phase the skis must be continually steered back uphill across the body and eventually underneath the body and into the next turn.

One of the most common errors occurs due to impatience, which greatly disrupts the timing. Many skiers are in a rush to come back down and make an early and abrupt 'down' motion. This abruptness again kills the turn and creates 'dead spots'. It causes the skis to over-edge and run straight, leaving telling 'rail' marks*. Once the skis are railing it is impossible to make a round turn or to link turns. Instead of connecting into the next turn smoothly, you are left to force the new turn by rotation and muscular effort. This is very fatiguing and lacks the flowing, dancing rhythm that makes powder skiing so fluid and graceful.

How positively you project depends on the conditions. If you are on the groomed piste and are connecting turns smoothly, you may not need a projection. The upper body (or hips) just flow uninterrupted into the new turn. But when skiing in more difficult conditions a positive forward and 'up' projection will be needed. If the snow is

* As in railway lines.

thick a positive projection will help free the skis and initiate the new turn. So how much you need to project depends on conditions and it is up to you to sense how much is needed and then apply the proper dose.

One of the finer skills required in deep snow is the ability to retract the feet. It is not needed in every turn*, but in the steep it is very useful for speed control. The key is to be relaxed and sensitive to the pressures underfoot. Towards the end of the turn as the pressure is building, the snow is trying to push your feet back up underneath you. In some conditions this feeling is very subtle, and at other times it is a stronger. At this precise moment, if you try to pull the feet up under you, with the help of the snow's gentle push, the retraction is easier than imagined. Unfortunately most skiers miss the moment. If you have a stiff bottom leg, or are too busy with an exaggerated or abrupt down motion, you will push right through the moment and be oblivious to the fact that the snow was trying to help you.

Helpful hints in the powder

- Remember to breathe. It is very easy to end up holding your breath, which makes it tiring and difficult to relax. I use a soft verbal 'boom', at the end of every turn. Besides forcing me to breathe it also helps develop a rhythm.
- Start with an uphill Christie (a turn back uphill – like the old-fashioned check, but rounder, smoother and progressive instead of abrupt). This allows you to create a moving platform and stabilise yourself in the 'ready position' before initiating the first turn. It also builds a little energy into the ski, which can be used to help release the initial turn. The

There is a little retraction in every turn when the feet come under the body and into the new turn. It is needed to ski off the bottom foot and allow the upper body to flow into the next turn. Here we are describing a conscious effort to retract the feet in a more exaggerated form. Refer back to Photos 35 in Plate section 3.

uphill Christie also gives you a millisecond test of the snow that can give you a vital clue of what to expect.

● Make the first turn count. Be positive. Use the uphill Christie to build a strong position from which to turn, and initiate the first turn with some purpose. If you nail the first turn you are off and running, full of confidence and prepared to find a rhythm. If you miss the first turn your confidence suffers and it can sometimes take the entire slope to pull things back together. When possible, start on your stronger side.

● Stand tall. Standing tall helps you to relax and reduce fatigue. It then leaves you with a full range of flexion and extension movements in the legs to absorb terrain changes, and to retract and extend when necessary.

● Keep your feet still in the snow. This allows you to equally weight both skis, or to delicately apply foot-to-foot pressure. 'Quiet feet' are a key to any type of skiing.

● Think 'slow motion'. Powder skiing is a slow motion event. Imagine yourself in a slow motion video. All your movements are purposeful, but slow and controlled.

● Be patient. Stay calm, take your time and allow the turn to develop. Wait until you are passing the fall-line before initiating a progressive down motion.

● Plant the poles. The poles are very important for timing and rhythm. A well-timed pole allows you to link turns. If your pole is late you will miss the moment. The pole also stabilises the upper body, and when you make a mistake the pole can give you a moment's grace to correct the problem before you fall over. A strong pole plant can allow you to uncross your tips, or help you wait for the skis to punch through into the next turn if you have hit some dense snow. Giles used to mark an 'x' in the snow and point to it and say, "Your pole goes there, or your face does!"

● 'Feel' the snow and adjust your radius of turn. Skiers often have a preconceived notion as to what radius of turn they are going to ski. If the snow is easy, any radius will do. But some conditions call for a shorter turn and others for a longer radius.

- Never 'congratulate' yourself while you are still in motion. You can hurt yourself just as easily during the last turn of a descent as you can somewhere in the middle of the slope. With the variations of snow found off-piste, many of which can be tricky, it is necessary to concentrate until you come to a complete stop.

Powder skiing on gentle terrain

If you have ever skied off-piste, you will know that sometimes the best snow is found on easy slopes. Other times you may seek security on gentle slopes while the steeper slopes may be prone to avalanche risk. Either way, you will spend some time skiing fresh snow on gentle terrain.

- Use 'bounce' generated from the ankles. You must feel the ankles working inside your boots.
- Positive forward and upward hip projection is a must.
- Let your skis do the work. Because the slope is gentle you will need some momentum. Do not finish the turns any more than necessary.
- Keep your feet still in the snow. Foot-to-foot pressure may be needed as compared to concentrating on equal weight.
- The bounce (and foot-to-foot pressure) will create energy in the ski. Use the rebound from the ski to help initiate the turns.
- Your rhythm will be quicker than on steeper slopes. Keep time with the hands and pole plant, and the bouncing ankle movements must be connected.

Often you will ski from a gentle slope into steeper terrain. Many skiers are caught off-guard at the transition. When you see the pitch about to change be ready to slow your movements down and complete your turns. The steeper slope will call for a much slower rhythm than the gentle slope, and much more completed turns.

Powder skiing on moderate terrain

Moving onto moderate terrain is the logical progression for powder skiers learning their trade. Experienced powder skiers will probably find themselves skiing moderate slopes most of the time. Moderate terrain is often easier to ski than gentle slopes because the increase in gravity helps the skis come through the turn much easier. And moderate terrain usually does not yet have the possible intimidation factor added to the equation. Here are some of the changes to think about when moving from gentle to moderate terrain.

- The rhythm will be slower than the bouncing rhythm of gentler terrain.
- As the pitch of the slope increases, so the pole plant will need to become firmer, and more important.
- You will need to steer the skis further across the fall-line, or make more complete turns than on gentler slopes.
- There will be times when you still have a connected 'bounce' and can use the rebound from the ski to help initiate the turns. But there will be times when you feel a need for retraction and extension. Retraction and extension is crucial for relieving pressure from the snowpack and controlling speed.

Powder skiing on steep slopes

See Photo series 45, Plate section 4.

We have all heard the term 'the steep and deep'. Here is where the intimidation factor can play a major part in one's performance. For those looking down a steep slope with fresh powder for the first time, trepidation is a natural reaction. For those who have a fear of heights, or steep slopes, it can be a constant inner struggle. If you are tense and frightened it will be difficult to apply yourself. But the only way to learn is to be put in the situation with the right conditions. I often say, 'each turn is one more turn in the bank'. You will build confidence with each experience and eventually, you may find yourself loving steep terrain. Here are some key points for skiing the 'steep and deep':

- Remember to breathe. It is very easy to hold your breath when you are tense.
- Think slow motion. The steeper the slope and deeper the snow, the slower your rhythm needs to become.
- Complete your turns and build a good platform. The further across the fall-line you steer the skis the slower you will go. You will also gain time in which to stabilise yourself and prepare a good platform. Do not initiate a turn until you feel comfortable in the last turn.
- Let go of the mountain. An accomplished powder skier can get the feeling of a controlled dancing 'free-fall'. The movements are connected and it is inspiring. But if you are not ready for the free fall effect and want a slower descent, let go, less edge and more side-slipping is needed. Try linking side-slips and you will be amazed at how much easier it is to control your speed. Once you feel in control intimidation is quickly replaced by exhilaration.
- A strong pole plant is critical. A firm pole plant will stabilise the upper body and help trigger the turn. It will also allow you to 'hang' on the pole for an instant if you make a mistake. This millisecond's grace can make the difference between correcting the problem and skiing into the next turn, or falling headfirst.
- Retract the feet. The steeper the slope and deeper the snow the more retraction will be necessary. Once you have developed the skill of retracting the feet you will have become a very accomplished powder skier.
- Extend. This naturally follows retraction in a connected rhythm. The combined effect of the two greatly influences speed control.
- Slough control. Whenever you ski a steep slope with fresh snow, the surface layers will slough. Do not be alarmed, as this is normal. If you feel uncomfortable with it, ski out to the

side and let the sliding snow pass. Once you become experienced with sloughing snow you will know how much you can safely safely handle, before needing to ski out to allow the sloughing snow to pass you by. When skiing the steep you not only have the powder snow in front of you to ski, but the added bonus of the sloughing snow as well.

The 'steep and deep' is not a necessary part of off-piste skiing. It can be avoided. But it is exciting. Your heart pounds away in your chest and the adrenalin is pumping. If you are introduced to steep, powder skiing properly, there is no reason for you to not become accomplished and comfortable on steep terrain.

Chapter Twelve

Skiing Spring Snow

PERFECTLY SMOOTH and softened spring snow is a real treat. But, because spring snow often does not get the chance to be created, or it gets skied too late in the day, days of 'real' spring snow are getting rarer. You will still get a day or two where conditions are what we call 'clean', but after that you need to start searching for it. This usually calls for a little physical effort.

In mid-March 1999 we had one of the best spring experiences I can remember.

The Val d'Isère-Tignes area was pretty tracked out and the prospect of finding 'clean' unmarked snow was a little depressing. It was definitely time to leave the resort and go for a walk. My group met at 8:15 and we piled into a mini-bus for the 25-30 minute trip to the neighbouring station of Ste-Foy. The plan was for an hour's hike up the ridge to the summit of the Foglietta. Normally we climb up the Foglietta for one reason only: to ski powder on the wonderful north facing bowl. But, today we had a different route in mind. We were going to ski the south side from about 2925 metres and eventually end up near Les Pigettes, situated at roughly 1450 metres on the road that leads back up to Val d'Isère. All in all, close to 1500 vertical metres of pristine spring snow.

We arrived in time to take the first chairlift of the day, and rode the three connecting lifts to the top of the station. We made our way to the ridge and prepared for our climb by shedding a layer of clothing and rigging our skis onto our backpacks. When everyone was ready we started our hike towards the summit.

It was a stunning day. Clear blue sky and crisp sunshine. And the views from the ridge were spectacular: Bourg St. Maurice and its

Hop Turn Series

Taken in the Col Pers.

Photo 42a:
Creating the 'ready' position.

Photo 42b:
Ready to go. In a low position and the pole has just been planted.

Photo 42c:
Springing up and jumping a few centimetres off the snow. All that is needed is a slight change of direction and a change of edges while airborne.

Photo 42d:
'Uncoiling' has produced the necessary change in direction. Landing in a high position on the new set of edges.

Photo 43a: *Getting that ski back on. Balance the ski with the toe in the toe-piece.*

Photo 43b: *Point the toes towards the sky while pressing down with the heel.*

Photo 44a:
Quiet feet. Both feet are totally still in the snow, allowing for equally weighted skis, or, precisely applied foot to foot pressure.

Photo 44b:
Panicky feet. When stepping about it is impossible to equally weight both skis or to delicately apply foot-to-foot pressure. In deep snow the over-weighted ski will dive leaving the skier in a precarious position.

Powder Series on Steep Slopes

Taken on the steeper upper slopes on the northern side of the Combe du Signal. The snow was light and skied in a controlled free-fall fashion.

Photo 45a:
Pole is in and upper body is beginning to project into the turn.

Photo 45b:
Upper body has come up out of the snow and the legs are extending. Both hands are visible.

Photo 45c:
Legs are out to the side and the skis are coming back across the fall-line. The left arm is still while the right elbow and wrist are bending and the pole is moving forward.

Photo 45d:
'Ready' again. The arms are wider than they would be on a gentler slope.

Photo 45e:
Well through the 'door'. Note the flatness of the skis as they come under the body and are steered towards the fall-line.

Photo 45f:
Extending the legs to the side. The extension helps maintain contact with the snow and pushes the skis deeper into the snow, which also helps slow you down. The movements must be connected, retraction into extension into retraction and so on, to avoid 'dead spots'. Dead spots make deep snow skiing very difficult, and fatiguing.

Series on Skiing Crud

Chris and I were not looking for this snow. We just happened to come across it. I thought I'd prepared myself; to be strong, positive, and make the first turn count. The snow was much more resistant than anticipated and I was ambushed in the first turn.

Photo 46a:
This is the third turn of the series, and I'm in slightly better shape than the previous two turns, but it still isn't pretty. The snow is definitely winning. I'm relying heavily on my pole while heaving my skis out of the snow.

Photo 46b:
A couple of turns further on and I've turned defence into attack. The pole has been prepared in advance of a strong pole plant to stabilise the upper body

Photo 46c:
'Ready' again.

Photo 46d:
Change of
tactics.
Retracting the
feet but keeping
them in the
snow.

Photo 46e:
Back on the
attack. I find
this an
interesting
series because
two different
tactics are used
to deal with the
crud. In the
earlier turns a
jump turn was
needed to get the skis out of the snow and free them so that they could
be pivoted. As the run continued I slowly regained control and went
from struggling to attacking. In the last few turns I was able to keep my
feet in the snow and retract and steer the feet.

Photo 47: *Touring in difficult conditions. As soon as the skiers lose the relief given by the rocks, they will confront white-out conditions. Expert skill and experience with map, compass, and altimeter is a must to travel in these taxing conditions.* Photo Jean Marc Pic.

Photo 48: *Using donkeys en route to the snowline in the High Atlas Mountains of Morocco.* Photo Jean Marc Pic.

already green valley below us, Mont Blanc and its massif, towering above all else to the north. Across the valley to the west, Mont Turia and Mont Pourri. And further south La Grande Motte and our domain spread out before us.

As we climbed, I noticed a fog rolling in across the valley floor. Everything below about 1900 metres was blanketed in a mist. It was incredibly beautiful, but the fog might mean skiing in flat light conditions for the last four to five hundred vertical metres of our descent. There would be enough relief from trees and old farmhouses to help in the route finding, but I would rather not have to deal with the added complication. Besides, the bottom of the descent had wonderful terrain and beautiful scenery, and plunging from brilliant sunshine into a whiteout tends to put a damper on the festivities. I was inwardly concerned about the mist, but it promised to be a warm day and I was hopeful that the fog would burn off before we skied down to that level.

After resting we started our ski down and I took the opportunity to tell my clients that this was *real* spring snow. This was how it is suppose to feel underfoot. The difference between 'clean' spring snow, and tracked spring snow is like night and day. My spirits were soaring as we skied down on the perfect velvety carpet. There was a micro-thin layer of ice that was raised about a centimetre off the surface. (You sometimes get this thin layer of ice. It is so thin you do not feel it and it has no effect whatsoever on your skis). As our skis passed through the ice it broke away and tumbled down the slope beside us. The dancing ice crystals made the most beautiful musical tinkling to accompany us down the mountain, and everyone skied and felt like a champion. As we lost altitude we needed to play with the exposures in order to remain on perfect snow. Face a little more towards the sun for a softer touch here, or angle away from the sun for slightly firmer snow there. We skied down the last pitch and when we came around the corner, the sea of fog had vanished!

We arrived at the fork where we still had a choice. Normal route, or climb? Are they too tired to traverse and climb another 20 minutes or so? The regular route lost altitude along a narrow path. Not really very interesting skiing. I asked them how they felt and gave a description of the Promised Land, a mere 20 minutes away. My sales pitch seemed to work as they unanimously replied, "more please".

The climb and traverse brought us from shade into bright sunshine and onto a long beautiful slope that lead down to the road far below. We had started the descent on a south slope at 2925 metres. Now we were much lower, at about 2300 metres, where it was also much warmer. Added to the fact that it was also over an hour since we started our descent, the day was really starting to heat up. The descent naturally took us onto a western slope, which would be needed to be able to continue skiing down to the valley floor on supporting spring snow. We still had variations in terrain giving us different exposures to work with, but the western exposure would make all the difference at the lower altitudes when we approached the road.

I checked my watch and our taxi was due in about 20 minutes, and we still had a long way to go. I took off and away we skied, non-stop for about fifteen minutes. I knew this terrain from summer walks. We were skiing through beautiful pastures that in summer are covered in a carpet of a hundred different types of wildflowers. We skirted around farmhouses and through snow covered vegetable gardens, over fences and down delightfully varied terrain. My clients were in heaven as we finally arrived at the road just above Les Pigettes. The snow had been exquisite. It had been totally 'clean' from the summit to the road 1500 vertical metres below. And the sun had softened it to perfection.

Our local taxi drivers have a knack of making you look good from time to time, and today my man played his part. Just as we arrived and started to side-slip down to the edge of the tarmac, Fred, on cue, wheeled in to pick us up. Direct from the edge of the road, straight into his cab, and twenty minutes later we were reminiscing about one of the best spring mornings in years, and washing it down with a cold beer. It doesn't get any better.

Spring snow tips

Spring snow, after a good freeze, is undoubtedly the most forgiving of all off-piste surfaces. You can approach it just as you would a perfectly groomed piste. You can make long or short radius turns. You can ski soft and gently. Or, providing you have an obstacle free slope in front of you, you may ski as dynamically as you like. But, as the support layer starts to weaken it all changes. And when the surface layer becomes fragile, spring snow is far from forgiving. It can suddenly become the most technically demanding of all surfaces to comfortably ski.

Fragile spring snow will support the skis without breaking, but not the pole. You will be able to punch your pole through quite easily. By analysing the force that it takes to punch the pole through the surface, an experienced person can make many decisions. You can judge how much time you have left on that exposure before the support layer melts and what exposure you should be looking for next. You can also judge whether or not you will be able to ski to the bottom of the slope without breaking through. This helps avoid tricky and dangerous skiing. Once the support layer has melted through, that spring surface becomes un-skiable.

You can also feel the support layer weakening underfoot. You can test the snow by bouncing up and down lightly. The snow may crack around your skis and collapse and sink a few centimetres. If you feel the snow collapse underfoot at the top of a slope, chances are it will not support to the bottom of the slope. If you are skiing too dynamically and on an edge, the tail of the skis will start to break the surface at the end of the turn. You can feel them gently starting to crush the surface. This is a warning to start to back off. As the support layer starts to weaken, you must start to ski less dynamically and on a flatter 'A' type ski. Instead of skiing from edge-to-edge, think about making longer turns and introducing some side-slip in each turn.

The technical challenge is to be able to ski without breaking and damaging the surface. When it becomes really fragile the goal becomes just staying on top and getting down safely.

- As the support layer weakens, widen your stance. This will increase the surface area that is supporting your body weight.
- Imagine yourself skiing on eggshells. Think light!
- All movements must be smooth and progressive. Any abruptness or over-edging will cause you to break through.
- Retract to relieve the snow of pressure when initiating the turn.
- The pivoting must be positive. Project, 'uncoil', and turn the feet.
- Stay tall and patient. Any early down motion will over edge the skis. Do nothing to stop the pivoting and let the skis slide.
- There must be some side-slip in each turn. The more fragile the snow, the more side-slip is necessary.

As the support layer weakens, there comes a time when pivoting becomes very delicate. What you try depends on how steep the slope is.

Skiing fragile, spring snow on gentle terrain

A stem turn is very effective if you are skiing relatively slowly. But, because the snow is fragile, you must avoid over pressuring the downhill foot while building your platform.

- Again progressive edging is the key. Try to create a platform with the least edge possible or, the flattest ski possible.
- Initiate the pole plant and project onto the new ski with the new ski sliding. The sliding action will help minimize the stress on the fragile support surface.

- Steer the previously weighted ski parallel to the new working ski. Take your time. The ski will want to come parallel after the fall-line. Because the support is weak, keep this ski partially weighted to help distribute the body weight. Keep more weight on the uphill foot if the snow is really fragile.
- Continue the pivoting, and side-slip as you complete the turn while gently preparing for the next turn.

A hop turn is also very effective if you are skiing a little quicker. Again, because the snow is fragile, the platform from which to hop must be created gently and progressively. You must land softly in a high position, and sliding.

Skiing fragile, spring snow on moderate terrain

A stem is still an effective approach on moderate terrain if you can create a platform without breaking through. The platform building stage is crucial as the downhill foot is being isolated because it is taking all the weight as the uphill foot is being stemmed uphill.

The retraction jump turn also works well. The classic jump turn will not work because of the lack of a support surface to push off from. Remember, the support layer is weak. Do not try to jump and pivot the skis all the way around. Just get the pivoting started. Land softly in a tall position, sliding, and continue to steer the skis.

Skiing fragile, spring snow on steep slopes

Unfortunately your options are limited on fragile snow in steep terrain. A stem doesn't work because too much pressure builds on the downhill foot and you will breakthrough. Your only chance of turning is the retraction jump turn. Creating the platform is a delicate operation, as is the retraction and pivoting, and the landing. It is imperative to land on both feet in a high position and sliding. If you land on an edge you will immediately breakthrough and fall.

Whether you are on gentle, moderate, or steep terrain, there comes a time when turning is next to impossible. The goal becomes just staying on top and getting to the bottom. Now your only hope is to side-slip. Widen you stance, diverge the uphill ski slightly, and weight both skis. Keep your feet as quiet as possible. Any extra movement can be enough to catch an edge. And the faster you can comfortably side-slip, so much the better, as a little speed helps you stay on top. Imagine yourself water skiing. You plane across the surface until you let go of the rope. Then as you slow down you sink deeper and deeper into the water. Speed has a similar effect on fragile snow (these tactics would be the same for fragile wind-blown snow).

The most important tactic in skiing spring snow is properly using the various exposures that a slope may give you, and understanding where to go next. You can change exposure to find firmer or softer snow. Gentle slopes hold differently from steeper slopes of the same exposure. Ask yourself: This gentle slope is perfect but what can I expect when I come to the steeper slope ahead? You must have a feel for what conditions at the top of a slope tell you about the conditions to be expected further down the mountain. Will it support? Will the support improve? How much longer will this exposure remain safe? Will it hold for another fifteen minutes, or for at least another half-hour? Knowledge of the terrain is critical. Can I change exposure farther down to find safe snow?

Much thought and experience need to go into skiing spring snow correctly and making the most of the conditions. It is a beautiful art.

Chapter Thirteen

Skiing in Other Conditions

Skiing crud

WHEN GUIDING clients, the last thing I want to do is drag them into crud, or breakable crust. I take pride in finding good snow, and ending up in crud is embarrassing. (TJ never skis crud. He describes the tough snow he finds as 'snow with surface tension'). But, no matter hard you try, you will find some difficult snow from time to time. Here are some pointers for snow with the dreaded 'surface tension'.

If the surface tension, or crust, is thin, you can sometimes ski through it, keeping your skis in the snow. But, it does however take good technique to deal with this type of snow. The stronger or deeper the surface tension, the better technique is required to ski through it normally. But eventually the surface tension will become so thick that it is impossible to ski and connect one turn into the next. When you arrive in the crud, try these pointers.

- Prepare yourself mentally. Be ready. You will need to be strong and dynamic. You will need to show the snow who is boss. If you go into it timidly and let the snow take over, you will find it rough going.
- The first turn is crucial. Use the uphill Christie. Because the snow is thick it will be more like a check. But you must link the movement into the first turn without hesitation.
- A strong pole plant will never be as useful as in crud. The skis will need time to punch through the thick snow and a stabilising, time-winning pole plant is a saviour.

- A strong projection is also needed to help free the skis.
- Link movements. Avoiding 'dead spots' is critical. Because the skis cannot move through and into the turn naturally, you will need to get them out of the snow. Use the rebound from the ski with a jump and a retraction to get the feet out of the snow. But on landing the feet must be turning in the direction of the new turn while the upper body remains facing the fall-line. And the feet must continue to turn back across the body throughout the 'down' motion. This will give you a maximum of upper and lower body independence, resulting in maximum 'uncoiling' to help get the next turn started. The turning feet will also help to build energy in the ski and create a rebound.

Skiing crud is hard work and challenging. If you can ski it well, it is very rewarding. If you do not have the technique for this type of snow, you are better off doing kick-turns and traversing. This type of snow can put the knees at risk and is better off being avoided.

Photo Series 46 in Plate section 4.

The steep

You have already picked up some tips for 'steep' terrain skiing in the previous sections, where jump and stem turns are always an option. Here are a few basic reminders for use in firm snow...

The first thing you want to think about when the going gets steep is to feel stable and under control. But how do you accomplish this?

- Widen your stance. As the terrain becomes steeper the feet come further apart. Also think about separating your hands and arms a little to aid your balance. You do not see many tight-rope-walkers with their arms close together.
- Think about a strong pole plant. The more extreme the pitch, the more important the pole becomes in stabilising the upper body and triggering the turn.

- Prepare yourself. Be ready mentally. You must be positive. And prepare a good platform before initiating your turn.
- Control your speed. Think of linking side-slips whether you have chosen jump or stem turns. Landing, or arriving on a hard edge, induces speed, and is difficult to control. From a controlled side-slip you can progressively increase your edge and create a stable platform.
- Finish your turn. If you feel you are going too quickly, do not turn. Many skiers feel they will slow themselves down if they turn. All that happens is that the skis are pointed downhill again, gravity takes over, and the situation worsens. Never turn until you feel controlled and comfortable in the last turn, especially on steep slopes.
- When in doubt – side-slip.

When traversing, side-stepping up, side-stepping down, or side-slipping on steep slopes, your uphill arm is of much better use if you hold the pole down from the handle. A lower grip gives you better leverage to push off from, and it brings the uphill arm into a more natural position from which to aid your balance.

It is of paramount importance in steep terrain to be aware of what lies below in the fall-line. Search out the safest fall-line possible and when obstacles are unavoidable, ski cautiously or side-slip. Your life may depend on it.

Flat light

What is flat light? Flat light conditions prevail when cloud cover, and possibly accompanying snowfall, diffuses the sunlight, thus prohibiting shadows from being cast. It makes it 'difficult to impossible' to see the contours of the terrain; all depending on how much light is getting through. (But, it can get worse. You can find yourself in a total white-out. All reference points disappear and all you can see is white; an incredibly disorientating and potentially dangerous situation.)

It's really no wonder that many skiers absolutely detest skiing in flat light, so much so that they'd prefer to take the day off and stay in the chalet. Others have discovered a quiet, private world that holds some of their favourite skiing memories. There is something special about skiing in falling snow that takes me back to childhood, and I always look forward to skiing during a snowfall.

We need snow to be able to ski, and if you want guaranteed sunshine on your holiday, a beach resort would be a safer bet. In the mountains you take what you get weather-wise, and to maximise the enjoyment of your holiday it is important to try to see the 'bright side' of skiing in flat light. It is a question of confidence, and the more you do it, the easier and more enjoyable it becomes.

One of the biggest problems with snowy days is trying to keep your goggles from misting over. Most inexperienced skiers have a bigger battle with their eyewear than the weather itself, and I think this has a lot to do with many skiers' dislike of such conditions. The problem often comes because skiers fall over, overheat while struggling to get up, and all of a sudden the storm going on inside their goggles is worse than the storm itself. The better you ski, the less you fall, and staying on your feet goes a long way in helping to keep the goggles clear. There is also an art to handling your eyewear so that they do not steam up. And persevering in flat light not only improves your skiing, but also gives you a chance to perfect the tricks needed to keep your goggles clear. Once you get a feel for handling your goggles and keeping your vision mist-free, the flat light itself poses much less of a threat.

The easiest place to start is in the trees. Whether you are on- or off-piste, trees give you relief that eliminates the problem of reduced visibility. You may not see as well as on a bright sunny day, but the visibility will still be good enough and not a major problem.

Powder skiing in the trees is totally different from the continuous rhythm type skiing used in open powder slopes. On a treeless powder slope, you find a radius of turn and a rhythm that you use in each turn, from top to bottom. In the trees you must be prepared to change radius and rhythm in each turn to avoid the trees. And it can become a bit of a ride-um-cowboy type of event as you deal with the deep snow, the slope, and choosing your route between the trees. The better spaced the trees, the easier it is to negotiate your route through the forest, but you must be technically good enough to control your speed and comfortably choose your line.

During the 1981-82 season I had one of my most memorable days ever while skiing the trees in a heavy snowfall. It had snowed most of the night and was still snowing huge flakes when I awoke that morning. My brother Dennis and I decided to head up to the Fornet cable car to spend the morning skiing in the forest. There we ran into T.J., who at the time was still with the E.S.F. but had a rare morning off, and his friend 'once-to-look' Russell. It was shaping up to be a classic day of skiing as we had great conditions and group of characters who were all strong skiers.

However, the day did not start out so well. For some unknown reason we decided to take the lift to the top, which was above the tree line where the visibility was basically zero. A real whiteout. T.J. was leading the way when he skied into an unseen dip and went head over heels, leaving both skis somewhere behind him. We gathered round and quickly found one ski but could not find the other. We searched for half-an-hour or so when T.J. finally said, "Forget it boys. You guys go on and I'll ski to the bottom on one ski". There is a saying that goes "There is no such thing as helping friends on a powder day" and we abandoned T.J. in a flash.

Dennis, Russell and I immediately dropped down into the trees and we were totally on our own. Today, during a snowfall every skier and boarder in town goes directly to the Fornet. But those many years ago, Val d'Isère was a different place, and we had the forest to ourselves. It was snowing incredibly hard, and each time we came back up it was difficult to see where our tracks had been. We would arrive at the top and then ski non-stop to the bottom, flying down between the trees and taking air wherever we could with snow spraying up over our heads. The three of us were beaming from ear to ear, and even the cable car operator was caught up in the mood. He would be waiting for us at the bottom, and the instant we arrived he would slam the doors shut and whisk us back to the summit. It was incredible to have our own private cable car and get this type of service. We skied until we were exhausted and to this day I cannot remember a better day's skiing in my entire life. Every year or so when Russell passes through town, our conversation at some stage always returns to that memorable day, and Russell always laughs and says, "Poor T.J.". To this day, that was the first, and last, ski my friend T.J. has ever lost.

Once you get above the tree line, skiing in flat light is a totally different story. Flat light can become a whiteout, where contours and the horizon disappear. It makes guiding much more difficult and the first task is to keep track of where you are. I usually choose a sector that I have skied recently where the terrain is fresh in my mind, so that I might recognise a rock, or a lone tree, or perhaps a patch of grass that has been exposed by the wind. These clues can help me picture where I am and imagine the terrain in front of me, which helps enormously in route finding. Although many areas are immediately eliminated because of terrain traps such as cliffs, holes or embankments, or undulating terrain, there are still other places that I feel comfortable to ski.

When confident of what lies below, I absolutely love the feeling of skiing into a white nothingness. It can be quite spooky skiing into what seems a vast void, but you get an incredible feeling of free falling. You must let your skis find the fall-line and your experience dictate the rhythm that the slope requires. You must stay relaxed and allow your motor memory to come up with the programmed movements, and let yourself go. For me, skiing in great snow in flat light in terrain I know and trust, is perhaps the ultimate feeling in skiing.

It is not unusual to have a client complain about the visibility, and my response is to ask he or she if they'd like to go first. The difference between going first and last in a group of six is like night and day. Once I ski down and stop before disappearing into the whiteness, I become a reference point, and the faint shadow of my track also helps. With each skier the visibility improves and the last person down has a much easier time than the first skier does. If you struggle in flat light, try hanging around at the back of the group, and the going will be easier.

Tips for flat light

Goggle control

The first thing I would recommend is to buy a good pair of goggles. Certain sunglasses may be fine in a fog, but because they do not have double lenses they steam up after a fall, and tend to mist up when stopping or when falling snow lands on them. A good pair of goggles will have better ventilation, and will pick out the relief in terrain much more effectively than a cheap pair.

Here are a few tips in keeping your vision as clear as possible.

- Once you put your goggles on, leave them on. They may steam up in a cable car or funicular, but they will clear once you get moving again. Constantly taking them off and putting them on almost always results in moisture getting on the inside of the lens, making it difficult to clear them.
- When putting your goggles on, avoid pulling them over a wet hat. This is most easily done by first carefully placing the goggles on your face in the proper position, then stretching the strap up and over the back of your head. Reverse the process to take them off. Hold the goggles in place while stretching and pulling the strap back over your head.
- You can try some of the various wipes and products that are supposed to help keep the lens mist-free. These are to be applied before you go out skiing.
- Carry a clean, absorbent cloth with you in case you need to wipe either the outside or inside of the lens.

- Take care of them. They scratch easily and if you crack the lens, condensation will get between the lenses and can render them useless.

Skiing in the trees

- **Ski under control.** Hitting a tree is no joke, especially headfirst. You will never win a battle against a tree.
- **Look ahead.** Besides choosing where your next turn should be, you must be aware of where that turn will lead you. Try to look at least two turns in front of you. Skiers often trap themselves against a tree or rock because they did not look far enough ahead, and were unaware of where their turn would take them (looking ahead is important in any terrain. Many skiers focus too closely in front of their tips).
- **Focus on the space between the trees.** People often concentrate on the trees themselves instead of the empty space between the trees. Remember, it is the spaces you are aiming for.
- **Ski with a buddy.** In Canada the heli-skiing outfits all insist that you ski with a partner in the trees. In case of a problem or accident, someone is there to help or to notify others of your location. This makes sense no matter where you may be skiing.
- **Beware of tree-wells.** If you are skiing somewhere like Canada where there can be an enormous depth of snow, beware of tree-wells that form around the bases. They can be 30 feet deep, and if you fall into one you could easily suffocate before being rescued. These tree-wells are the main reason behind the buddy system at CMH.
- **Stop if you lose visibility.** This may sound obvious, but it is very tempting to keep going when you have a good run going. If you take a face full of snow and can't see, don't risk it hoping that the snow sticking to your goggles is going to conveniently fall off.

- **Remove your pole straps.** Eliminate the possibility of damaging a thumb, wrist, elbow, or shoulder because you caught a basket on a branch or stump. If you let go of your poles every time you fall, weigh up the pros and cons and make a choice.

Above the tree line

Skiing above the tree line is real flat-light skiing. In the trees you still have relief and very good visibility, above the tree line is a totally different world. It can be so white that some people feel physically ill and it is not uncommon to feel slightly dizzy (If you think this sounds bad, try it with a hangover). This type of flat light skiing is not recommended unless you are a competent powder skier, have absolute confidence that the slope to be skied is smooth and obstacle-free, and you can navigate back to safety.

- **Have an intimate knowledge of the slope.** It must be smooth and hold no surprises.
- **Relax and breathe.** Being relaxed is always important for performance in any sport, and skiers naturally tighten up in flat light. Take some deep breaths before starting and remember to breathe on the way down.
- **Watch the skier in front of you.** You can get a good idea of the smoothness of the slope by watching their legs. If they have smooth uninterrupted movements, chances are the slope is flat.
- **Stop the leader.** I will have a good idea of how far I can ski before disappearing into the whiteness beyond, but I tell my skiers to alert me when I'm about to go too far. If the leader skis out of sight, they are no longer a valuable reference point, which gives a little relief to help guide the others down.
- **Make the first turn count.** This is advice I would give in any situation, but a positive start is especially important in flat light. Start with an uphill Christie, and make a strong, positive initiation to the first turn.

- **Stand tall.** It is easy to crouch down in flat light and this compresses the body like a spring. If you do hit something, because you are compressed there is no absorbing movement available in the legs. Even a small bump can cause an unnecessary shock. If you are standing tall there is a full range of leg movement to cushion the shock of an unseen bump, and to retract and extend when necessary. (Standing up makes it easier to relax. If you are relaxed you would be amazed at how much you can absorb. But if you are tense the shock is magnified).

- **Let your skis find the fall-line.** Because you can't see the fall-line, you can only guess. Picture the fall-line in your mind, relax, push off when you are ready, and then be receptive to the pull of gravity. Finding the fall-line does become easier with practice.

- **Link your movements.** This is where your experience comes in. You must trust your programmed motor skills to find the radius of turn and the rhythm that the slope and snow conditions dictate. Once you've found the tempo, the movements must be linked, and repetitious. If you have "dead spots" in your movements it is impossible to link turns, and then every turn becomes the first turn, which is seriously hard work.

- **Plant your poles.** A positive pole plant can help you find and stay in a good rhythm; as well as stabilize the upper body. In flat light, you can use all the help you can get.

- **Let it go, and let it flow.** It's all about being relaxed, confident, and positive. Have a positive attitude, find a flowing rhythm, and let yourself go.

Chapter Fourteen

Touring

TOURING IS RAPIDLY increasing in popularity as more and more people are skiing off-piste, and resorts are being skied out much quicker than in the past. Touring is a great way of getting just that little bit further away to find untracked snow and separate yourself from others who are skiing off-piste. And for the more serious, it is possible to get miles away for days at a time. Either way, touring is a great addition to off-piste skiing, and the choice of terrain and destinations is almost limitless.

Photo 28, Plate section 2.

There are many ways to go about touring, and at Alpine Experience we use variations of touring as a regular option for our clients. The Val d'Isère - Tignes area offers an excellent range of tours and we do our best to take advantage of the conditions, terrain, and scenery. Touring, however, does not need to be as demanding as one might imagine. It is possible to tour for just the morning and still be back down in time for lunch. In a few hours it is possible to choose routes that assure easy walking and gentle skiing for skiers who are less fit or new to touring, or tougher walks and demanding skiing for the fit and experienced. From the resort there are many day-tours available as well, again varying in degrees of physical effort and technical difficulty, where you are out all day long and back to the comfort of your chalet for the evening.

Soft-core touring

These types of tours are for those whom I would describe as soft-core tourers. Those who walk from time to time in search of untracked snow when fresh snow is scarce, or to reach a special run that is accessed only by a walk. Occasional tourers may walk just for a change of pace or the exercise, or for peace and quiet when the resort is full. This type of touring still gives you a feel for the walking technique, a sense of accomplishment for the physical effort put in, and a feeling that you have earned your solitude and fresh snow. It gives you the satisfaction of arriving on top of your chosen peak and enjoying the stunning vista and a well-deserved picnic. And at the end of a great and rewarding day out you can enjoy a beer at your favourite bar and the comfort of your own bed.

Besides the home comforts, soft-core touring has the possibility of using your own equipment. Touring boots, bindings, and skis are much lighter than normal downhill equipment and are very necessary on longer tours. But they are more difficult to ski, and, for an inexperienced off-piste skier, can be a nightmare if the snow is tricky. On a morning or day tour, because you are walking uphill for a far shorter time, the lightness of equipment is not as important as it is for multi-day tours, and you can use your own skis and boots with adapter bindings. These 'adapters' can be fitted into normal bindings and give you the same heel lift function as a touring binding. 'Skins', which are now synthetic, are attached to the sole of your skis and they allow you to walk uphill. The direction the 'fur' lies in is such that it allows the ski to slide forward, but when you put your weight down to slide the other ski forward, the fur stops the weighted ski from sliding backwards. The 'skins', combined with the heel action of the binding, makes walking uphill not only possible, but fairly effortless. Once at the top you remove the adapters and 'skins' and put them in your backpack, and you are ready to step into your bindings and enjoy the precision of your own boots and skis.

There are, however, a few drawbacks with the adapters that I should warn you about. They are heavy and do take up a lot of space in your backpack. Adapters can also be a little temperamental when trying to snap them into the existing bindings and seem to need a bit of tape from time to time to keep them functioning. And, because you are on top of your regular bindings, you get the feeling you are wobbling around in high-heels (Not that I know what wearing high-heels feels like). This added height can give an unsteady feeling when climbing steep slopes or doing up-hill kick-turns. But my colleague, Jean-Marc, has come up with a solution to this problem.

Because the new touring bindings are much stronger than they used to be, and because of their improved release mechanisms, he has mounted his everyday skis with touring bindings. He feels confident enough with them (he never falls) to ski them daily and then have the touring option when needed. Seeing this, many of my clients have bought off-piste type skis, and mounted them with touring bindings. This eliminates the hassle of the adapters, and gives them a far easier and safer ski than a touring ski for the descent. I would recommend this as a great option for occasional tourers as a touring set-up. I wouldn't recommend anyone but a true expert to ski on touring bindings on a daily basis because, even though they have made great strides in improving the release mechanism, they are not as smooth as traditional bindings.

Many people seem to like the sound of staying in a mountain refuge or hut, but are not too sure if they want to stay away for an entire week. Two of my other colleagues, Pietro Barigazzi and Olivier Carrère, often take skiers out on two-day tours that include one night away in a refuge. This type of tour has several advantages. Normally when skiers book a holiday it includes lodging for a week, and a two-day tour means you only need to spend one night away from pre-paid accommodation. If you are planning a two-day tour you also have the option to wait and watch the weather, and to go when conditions are optimal as good weather makes a tour so much more enjoyable. If you are thinking about signing up to tour for a week or longer, but are not too sure how you would cope in a refuge, a night away is a great chance to find out if refuge life suits you before taking the plunge.

Longer tours

Once you get into multi-day tours, it becomes much more serious. With morning or day tours, you have a very good idea of what is in store weather-wise and, if you do not like the forecast, you can simply choose not to go. On a multi-day you don't have this luxury. If, on a seven-day tour, the weather 'socks in' on day four, you may need to stay put in the refuge and wait for the weather to clear. Or, you may need to travel and ski in a total whiteout. It takes unshakeable confidence, plus enormous skill with a compass and altimeter, to safely travel in flat light conditions, and not everyone is willing to tackle such a challenge. If you are planning to go on a long tour, you must be prepared to sit tight and weather out a storm, or be prepared to travel in difficult conditions. And you must have someone guiding you who can navigate in the worst weather conditions imaginable.

Jean Marc was touring locally several years ago when he came up against some really bad conditions. It was warm and had rained most of the night, which meant there was no freeze and the snowpack would be suspect. His route would need to be chosen accordingly. There was also a low-lying fog. Visibility would be basically zero and the compass and altimeter work would need to be spot on. All in all, a nasty combination of factors for the team to deal with.

Jean Marc was well aware of the pounding rain during the night, and he awakened his troops early to ensure a good start on a difficult day. When they left the Refuge de la Femma that morning the mist was down and humidity hung in the air. They were heading to the Col de Pierre Blanche, down into the Vallon de la Leisse, then to the Col de la Vanoise and the Refuge Félix Faure. Jo Moss was there that day, and here is how she remembers the adventure.

"Water was dripping everywhere. The snow was wet and stuck to the bottom of our skis in great clumps so that we had to plod along instead of slide. A section that should have taken 45 minutes took over two hours. It really was tough going. Jean Marc turned the situation around by explaining how he was navigating. None of us

When snow is scarce, or just for the ride, heli-skiing is an option. This photo shows heli-skiing in Sweden during late-May, where it is possible to ski under the midnight sun. The helicopter was older than I was.

had really appreciated the skill involved. Using the map he showed us how misleading a compass could be in these conditions and explained the importance of the altimeter, and the co-ordination between the two. He managed to change the entire focus of the walk from incredibly hard work into a concentrated learning session.

"Jean Marc asked us to spread out during the climb, even with the poor visibility. Inwardly, he must have been very concerned, but his calm, matter of fact approach to the situation made us all relax. I felt totally safe in his hands. Even though we couldn't see a thing, I knew he would find the way. He calmly kept checking the map, compass, and altimeter, and kept the group involved by asking us to check our bearings as well.

"It was quiet and wet, and we were all very aware of the snow conditions. We continued climbing, and eventually the ground started to level out underneath us as we were nearing the Col. Jean Marc had brought us to exactly the right place to cross over to the other side.

Amazing! We were all relieved to be at the summit and sat down for a much-needed chat about our climb and to enjoy a rest. After some tea and chocolate we started to prepare for our journey down the other side and on towards the Col de la Vanoise and the Refuge.

"Suddenly some sunlight broke through the clouds long enough for us to appreciate where we really were. We all took some photos and absorbed the lay of the land before us, before plunging back into the heavy mist. Jean Marc still had some serious work in front of him. Some in the group who had never been in these taxing conditions were now much more relaxed. After seeing Jean Marc guide them so precisely to the Col, their anxiety just seem to evaporate. We were guided down safely to the shelter, and it was a day none of us will ever forget."

See Photo 47, Plate section 4.

Because of the unstable snow conditions Jean Marc had not only needed to protect the group from avalanches but also to avoid spending time under steep slopes. If he had missed the proper place to pass the Col, the group could have ended up against an impassable rock wall, or fallen over an unseen cliff.

On to the refuges

The refuges themselves vary from very basic dormitory-type rooms cramped with sweaty people, with outhouses perched on the edge of cliffs and minimal washing facilities, to rather comfortable huts such as the Femma that boast showers with hot and cold water, and toilets. These 'Femma' type refuges are rare, but newly built refuges are much more comfortable than the old ones and have improved sanitation.

The refuges are usually manned and the cooking is done for you. This saves needing to carry your own food and, after a long day, it is nice to have a meal served up for you. The food in refuges also varies, from acceptable to very good.

Conserving energy is very important on a long tour making good touring equipment a necessity. Touring boots, skis, and binding are much lighter than regular downhill equipment, and their 'lightness' is very noticeable and beneficial while climbing. The skis are also shorter; making the necessary uphill kick turns much easier. Unfortunately there is a downside to touring equipment. The lighter skis are more 'nervous' than regular skis and can be very difficult in tricky snow. They tend to jump around and do not punch through thick snow and this can make a skier feel very uncomfortable. The light boots do not have the same rigidity as downhill boots and lack control in comparison. Added to the lighter bindings, the whole package is much more difficult to ski than regular equipment. But, touring equipment is in the middle of a revolution and is drastically improving. The skis are now slightly wider than touring skis of the past and new materials are helping to make them less 'nervous'. The boots are stiffer, and the bindings are stronger with an improved release mechanism. If you are planning on a long tour, make sure you rent or buy the latest equipment possible.

On a multi-day tour, terrain can be unfamiliar and you are a long way from help if something goes wrong. Knowing the limitations of your group is always significant but never more so than on a long tour. When climbing, you must consider the reserves of the weakest, and walk at a pace that will not only get them through the day, but the remaining days as well. The importance of choosing the best snow is exaggerated because the skiing is trickier with touring equipment, and you don't need a knee injury way out in the backcountry. Group harmony is crucial because not only are you walking and skiing all day with the same people, but you must eat and sleep with them as well. As I said, multi-day touring is much more serious and the dynamics of it all are more complicated, but for some skiers, it is the only way to go.

The destinations for multi-day touring are almost limitless. Anywhere you find snow and mountains, such as Canada, America,

South America, New Zealand, Australia, India, Europe, or Northern Africa, to name a few. Many countries have networks of huts or refuges and, where these are unavailable, the hard-core tourers will build their own shelters in the snow. There are possibilities in places most people wouldn't imagine. Jean-Marc, Pietro and Olivier regularly take groups to the High-Atlas Mountains of Morocco, which top out at over 4,000 metres, and Turkey, and are busy planning a trip to the Andes.

Photo 48, Plate section 4.

Tips for touring

- Walk at an easy pace. It is crucial to conserve energy and the best way to do that is to pace yourself. Walk at a pace you could keep up all day if necessary, because you never know when you might need to push yourself to your extremes. If someone gets injured it might be necessary to go for assistance that could be a long way off, or you may need your energy to build a snow hole and spend the night. Someone may become exhausted and you may need to go back down and carry his or her equipment. All sorts of situations can arise that may call for you to be strong, and climbing too quickly is the surest way to drain away your strength. Climbing always eats away some of your energy, and with it, some co-ordination as well. People never ski as well after a climb, and if you've pushed yourself too hard on the way up, you will pay with a poorer skiing performance on the way down. Touring equipment is more difficult to ski anyway, and if you combine that with fatigue and the possibility of tricky snow, you have a combination that could lead to injury. Remember, pace yourself.
- Try to keep your skis in the snow and slide them along as you climb to help conserve energy. Inexperienced tourers often lift their skis out of the snow and this is much more fatiguing.

- Make sure you use the proper equipment. Adapters are fine for short tours but it is important to have skis short enough to allow you to execute a comfortable uphill kick turn. For longer tours, touring skis, boots, and bindings are a must but as I said before, the equipment is improving and it wouldn't hurt to search out the latest. Breathable clothing is also essential, and having zippers under the armpits and full-length zippers on the trousers for ventilation gives you welcome options for regulating your body temperature.

- Master uphill kick-turns. These kick-turns are a necessity and do take some practice, but once you get the hang of it they are relatively easy. The uphill kick turn is safe because if you fall, you will fall into the mountain with your stomach on the snow and your feet below you, and you are in a perfect position to execute the self-arrest. All that is needed is a press-up and you will stop immediately. The downhill kick-turn, which I ask my clients to avoid, is dangerous because you are in a position where you will fall downhill headfirst with both legs pointing in opposite directions, and it is almost impossible to stop from that position.

- Make sure your boots fit. If you are renting (or buying), make sure your boots are not too big. You would be surprised at how many skiers are sold ski boots that are much too large for them, and it is the most common problem I come across when people complain about their feet. Skiing is one thing, extended periods of walking is another, and a good fit is essential. Always carry 'second skin' as blisters can develop even in well-fitting boots, and if you don't need the 'second skin', I can guarantee that someone else will.

- Carry energy food and hydrating fluids. You dehydrate very quickly in the mountains and regular water-stops and food-breaks are a must to maintain your strength.

- You must include your standard safety equipment on top of the extra things you may need to carry.

- Avoid over-heating. Over-heating drains your energy and is very dehydrating. Take off some clothes and walk slowly so that you do not sweat too much, but be ready to put clothes back on anytime you stop for a break, and especially at the summit where you are often exposed to wind. Be aware of wind direction so that you can shelter yourself on the lee side when stopping to rest.

● Do not be overly ambitious. It is important to know your physical limitations and not attempt tours that are beyond you, whether it is a question of conditioning or skiing ability. It is not necessary to be super fit or experienced, but you should tour to your fitness and technical levels. Out in the middle of the mountains is no place to injure yourself, or collapse physically or mentally. If you ski regularly with a professional, he or she will know your limitations and choose an itinerary that suits you. If you are skiing with someone who does not know your limitations, play safe and refrain from over-dressing your capabilities.

Final Tracks

I truly hope that you have found this book informative and enjoyable. Hopefully my love of the mountains and off-piste skiing has come across in these pages, and the book has been an inspiration to you. Off-piste skiing has been a major part of my life. Hopefully I'll still be spending my winters skiing in the mountains when I'm eighty years old. And hopefully you will still be skiing as well.

The off-piste domain is one of the most beautiful places on earth. The scenery is absolutely breathtaking. Also, the mood of the mountains is always changing, and no two days are ever the same. Add to this, the quiet peacefulness, which has an incredible clarity, and the whole ambience is uplifting.

You can also feel the power of the mountains, which makes travelling and skiing in this environment incredibly exhilarating and stimulating. Learning to handle yourself in these surroundings breeds a feeling of accomplishment and leaves you with memories that will last a lifetime.

But if some of the stories and photographs have dampened your enthusiasm towards skiing off-piste, I do not apologise. If your eyes have been opened to the possible risks, and you are not convinced that the risks can be reduced to an acceptable level, I feel I've accomplished part of what this book is about. Off-piste is not for everyone. We all have our own level of risk acceptability. It is up to all of us to decide for ourselves what is acceptable, and what isn't.

For everyone with an interest in off-piste skiing, whether you are wanting to try it for the first time or are already a confirmed off-piste skier, I hope you have found some guidelines within these pages. Hopefully you will feel the need to take it seriously, and to approach it properly. Just being in the mountains is incredibly liberating. And to be able to ski off-piste is nothing short of a privilege.

This has been a labour of love. I'm not a snow scientist. And I'm not a world authority on avalanches. There are many people who know much, much more about these subjects than I do. But, what I have learned over the past twenty years about skiing off-piste, I gladly share with you.

T.J. and me surveying our choices along a ridge above the Chardonnet.

Acknowledgements

I'd like to take this opportunity to thank my good friend and colleague Chris Souillac, for his time and expertise that have gone into the photographs for this book. Chris' photos have already appeared in various magazines around the world, and this is his third book. He was also an instrumental figure in the founding of Alpine Experience.

Thanks also go to T.J.Baird who has readily offered his friendship, knowledge and experience, and Jean Marc Pic whose expertise and calm attitude in the mountains are a lesson to us all. Olivier Carrère and Pietro Barigazzi deserve a mention for their skills and unique senses of humour, which have helped make the company what it is today.

I would also like to thank Rob Cochran for his encouragement and constructive input during the writing of this book. Thanks also to Gill Onslow who, besides proof-reading, has put up with my moods over the last few months.

Finally, I would like to thank all of our clients who have placed their trust in us over the years.